speculates that, given the power of science to alter our existence, God should be able to do the same, but perfectly and eternally. Clark even suggests that, given the power that modern society has discovered, we can rationally conclude that the end of all things is probably not too far away.

Overall, Clark adopts the pose of one of the prophets he seems to declare redundant. In an age in which Christians in Western society are suffering an endemic lack of confidence, it is good to read such a robust defence of Christian theism. I doubt if he will convince Richard Dawkins; but he does expose the dogmatism, and credulity, of those who boldly declare there is no rational case for the existence of God.

Peter Forster is the Bishop of Chester.

GOD, RELIGION AND REALITY

STEPHEN R. L. CLARK

First published in Great Britain 1998
Society for Promoting Christian Knowledge
Holy Trinity Church
Marylebone Road
London NW1 4DU

British Library Cataloguing-in-Publication Data
A catalogue record for this book is available from the British Library

ISBN 0-281-05133-X

Typeset by David Gregson Associates, Beccles, Suffolk
Printed in Great Britain by J W Arrowsmith Ltd, Bristol

CONTENTS

_____

Acknowledgements

Some material embodied in this book has been published in assorted journals and collections, and is recycled (and amended) with the permission of the editors: 'Descartes' Debt to Augustine', M. McGhee, ed., *Philosophy, Religion and the Spiritual Life* (Cambridge University Press: Cambridge 1992), pp. 73–88; 'Where have all the Angels gone?', *Religious Studies* 28.1992, pp. 221–34; 'Orwell and the Anti-Realists', *Philosophy* 67. 1992, pp. 141–54; 'Natural Goods and Moral Beauty', D. Knowles & J. Skorupski, eds., *Virtue and Taste: Essays on politics, ethics and aesthetics in memory of Flint Schier* (Blackwell: Oxford, 1993), pp. 83–97; 'Substance, or Chesterton's Abyss of Light', *Proceedings of the Aristotelian Society Supplementary Volume* 95.1995, pp. 1–14; 'Objective Values, Final Causes', *Electronic Journal of Analytical Philosophy* 3.1995, pp. 65–78 (http://www.phil.indiana.edu/ejap/); 'How Chesterton Read History', *Inquiry* 39.1996, pp. 343–58; 'A Plotinian Account of Intellect', *American Catholic Philosophical Journal* 71.1997, pp. 421–32; 'Pantheism', David E. Cooper & Joy A. Palmer, eds., *Spirit of the Environment* (Routledge: London 1998), pp. 42–56; 'Berkeley's Philosophy of Religion', Kenneth Winckler, ed., *Companion to Berkeley* (Cambridge University Press, forthcoming).

Lines from John Buchan's poem 'Stocks and Stones', from his book *The Moon Endureth* (Thomas Nelson: Edinburgh 1923), are reprinted by permission of A. P. Watt on behalf of The Lord Tweedsmuir and Jean, Lady Tweedsmuir. Lines from G. K. Chesterton's poem 'Ecclesiastes', from his *Collected Poems* (Methuen: London 1923), are reprinted by permission of A. P. Watt on behalf of The Royal Literary Fund.

PREFACE

My aim is to show that there are good philosophical reasons for theism, and Christian theism in particular. It is widely supposed, even by believers, that this cannot be true. Some commentators dismiss theism as one failed theory amongst many. Others suggest that it can only be a recipe for a moral or a spiritual life, without any claim to 'truth in fact'. Others argue that it can be rationally adopted as a true account of things, but not for any reasons that philosophers can offer. Yet others declare that 'reason' and 'religion' are at odds, and that religion is the right, though quite irrational, response. All four schools have reasons, of a kind, for what they say, but all (or so I shall contend) are wrong. There are good reasons to believe that theism is the right response, and that traditional arguments have been misjudged.

What I shall offer are indeed traditional reasons for being a Christian theist: many are good reasons for being a theist even of another kind. The familiar labels (ontological, cosmological, teleological, moral) for general theistic arguments (familiar amongst non-Christian theists too) now disguise enormously many variations, both serious and scholastic, and what follows is not a survey of those variations. It may indeed sometimes be hard to see exactly which 'traditional argument' is intended – just because there have always been more arguments, and versions of each argument, than are now remembered. Most are not now understood, partly because the very label, 'God', misleads. To understand what 'God' means, we must follow through the arguments, and see what it is that they establish.

Like other 'natural theologians' (those, that is, persuaded that rational argument can be rightly used to clarify and demonstrate the truths of theism) I concede that not all Christian (or Jewish or Islamic) credal claims are provable 'by reason'. This is not to say that they are 'contrary to reason'. My claim, however, is that far more can be established than is commonly supposed: whereas

Aquinas thought that God's existence could be demonstrated, but not the doctrines of the Trinity and Incarnation, I regard these too as necessary postulates of reason. It follows that I side with those who make the startling claim that even atheists, as long as they are rational ones, rely on Christian axioms, on theorems that would not be true if Christian theism – or something very like it – weren't. There are those (including theists) who believe that this amounts to saying that atheists, or non-Christians, are irrational: that is not the point. Consider this analogy: we have at the moment no clear reason to believe or disbelieve (for example) Goldbach's Conjecture (that every even number larger than two is the sum of two prime numbers), but anyone who reasons mathematically is actually, though unknowingly, committed to one answer or the other. That is to say, there is a truth which no finite intelligence need know it knows: it is not irrational to disbelieve what we have not yet proved is true (nor yet to believe it, if there seems good reason to). The mathematical example permits a further gloss. As either Goldbach's Conjecture or its denial is a truth which transcends both our present knowledge, and any material instantiation, the present being of the truth is best explained as one of the thoughts of God. If there were no God, it could not now be *true* (as some acknowledge). If rational discourse is only possible in a God-directed universe, it follows that rational atheists must actually rely upon the truth of theism even to argue against it: this is not to say that atheists are incapable of rational thought, but only that – perhaps forgivably – they miss the implication of their own practice. I don't expect that any atheists (or any non-theists) reading this will readily be convinced of it: that is not how conviction comes. I do hope that a careful reading of the reasons will clarify what theists must, and do, believe.

Briefly: Christian theists acknowledge that there is a Truth wider than our conception of It, which demands our worshipful attention; that Its nature is such that It needs no further explanation; that It is such that we can reasonably think we might find out about It; that It is One, and therefore immaterial; that It must actually and entirely be what, intermittently, we are – that is, conscious; that It contains the standards for each finite being; that there must somewhere be something that is at once completely human and completely God; that It is threefold (being One, Intellect and Spirit); and that the whole community of Its creation is eternally contained in It.

These claims are ones that I have, variously, made before, together with other analyses of natural religion, ethics and epistemology. My chief works on the subject have been *From Athens to Jerusalem* (Clarendon Press, Oxford, 1984), *The Mysteries of Religion* (Blackwell, Oxford, 1986), *Civil Peace and Sacred Order* (Clarendon Press, Oxford, 1989), *A Parliament of Souls* (Clarendon Press, Oxford, 1990), *God's World and the Great Awakening* (Clarendon Press, Oxford, 1991), *How to Think about the Earth: models of environmental theology* (Mowbrays, London, 1993), and sundry papers.

Any philosophical contribution to these issues suffers one enormous burden: the burden, exactly, of philosophical commentary over two and a half millennia. What follows is not a survey, nor a summary. I have made no attempt to produce a bibliography of books and articles on these particular issues, still less to enter all the labyrinthine paths that open out from every sentence. Philosophical or natural theology is exceptionally rich in issues, and has been the source of many arguments that have borne fruit in philosophical psychology, logic, meta-ethics, aesthetics, epistemology, philosophy of science and moral or political discussion. This monograph is limited: a brief account of arguments I think sufficient to confirm the status of theological realism as a postulate of reason.

No doubt I have made many errors, despite the efforts of my friends (especially Gillian Clark and Michael McGhee) – and foes. No doubt I have often only echoed what my mentors say (amongst whom I identify Aristotle, Plotinus, Augustine, Descartes, Berkeley, Chesterton and Murdoch). My thanks to them, and also to other colleagues, friends and students, including Simon Hailwood, Patrick Quinn, Soran Reader, Paul Rooney and Panayiota Vassilopoulou.

Stephen R. L. Clark

University of Liverpool
1998

ONE

RELIGIOUS OBSERVANCES AND THEORIES

Our World and the Real World and Religion

RELIGION IS THE name we give to the rituals, recitations, social exchanges, calendrical observances and so on that we, variously, employ to keep our spirits up, confirm ourselves in our identities or help us through hard times. This rag-bag of observances may include whatever helps us to feel properly war-like, amorous, sociable, obedient, courageous, honest or ordinarily hard-working. Whether the spirit that is evoked through participation in the rites (say, the spirit of aggressive patriotism or dedicated scientific enquiry) has any existence apart from the participants' enspiritedness is often unimportant. Some will say, if pressed, that it does, that the rites 'literally' invoke it; others will agree that it does not, and wonder why this matters. It follows that people can be 'deeply religious', heavily and persistently involved in religious observances, without 'believing' in any god's existence outside the human breast. 'Religion' or even 'theology' would not vanish from the world even if we were all convinced – somehow – that atheists were correct 'in fact'. We might as easily or plausibly imagine that we would blow up all church organs, or only perform 'secular' music. Such a transformation would itself be a 'religious' revolution (and one of an entirely familiar, iconoclastic kind).[1]

Even those rites which are reckoned 'magical' are not always, and by all participants, expected to have direct effects on 'the real world'. People dance to mark the start of the rainy season, or before the harvest – but not necessarily to ensure the rain or harvest. They may know that rain or harvest will happen (or not happen) anyway, whether they dance or not, and yet still dance. Such rituals may express our hopeful expectations, or summon our courage to encounter danger, without anyone's supposing that they have effects upon the weather. Or rather: the effect they have is to mark out, or bless, the weather. Sometimes the distinction may be vague: a healing ceremony may actually help to heal, simply because the patient feels it should. Being blessed, the patient may recover – but the ceremony would still recur even if its only effect was on the patient's 'attitude', and even if its only effect was ceremonial. Rituals also divide our lives into convenient segments: childhood, adolescence, marriage, and retirement. Sometimes those rituals do consciously invoke some divine blessing; sometimes they express a gratitude, or pride, or sadness, that seeks for an ideal object; sometimes they are only parties – with this proviso, that after the party our duties and responsibilities are changed.

This contrast between 'the real world' and 'the human world' is itself an artefact. Until we realized, or decided, that there was a world outwith the one we made, no one could have answered, or even asked, the question whether religion was true 'in fact' or only (like other human institutions) 'by convention'. Galileo relied upon that contrast when he disproved, by thought alone, the Aristotelian claim that heavier things fall faster. It is in fact quite true that here on earth a pencil and a sheet of paper (say) will fall at different speeds. What Galileo saw was that this could not be the real case, that it must – as Aristotle himself suspected – be an effect of air-pressure: one two-pound weight can fall no faster – in a vacuum – than two one-pound weights, or else we could make things fall faster just by renaming them. The distinction long preceded Galileo: Democritos, father of both the atomic theory and social contract theory, said that 'really there are only atoms and the void: all else is by agreement'. Whether anyone made that same distinction earlier, who knows? It is always easy to forget it (and indeed present-day anti-realists[2] have made it their commitment to forget it). Our human world really is constituted by our words: we make new entities (as cities, families or corporations) by the power of words; we make and unmake laws and money, irrespective of what happens 'by nature'. 'With words the world was called out of the empty air':[3] but no words of ours created the real world. Realizing the reality of that nature, the world that we can't unmake by a word, we can equally imagine that Someone's words *might* work. But even if our words don't affect the world of 'atoms and the void', they will affect our world, the world that we experience, for good or ill. Very few of us are really prepared to live outside that human frame: the attempt to do so, once again, is likely to be founded in some ascetic religion for which merely human institutions have no force. In the human world there are privileged places, moments, classes: the gods (perhaps) think otherwise.

Even 'theology' would not vanish even if we 'knew' that atheists were right: that is, people would continue to tell stories about gods, and even seek to make them more or less compatible. Lacking any sense that 'the real world' was anything but vastly alien, they might tell *more* stories. They might not, of course, be entirely clear that this is what they were doing. Popular entertainment from television soaps to Tolstoy creates 'larger than life' characters in whose adventures we can be involved, and whose life-style we may hope to emulate. Even if we all 'know' that there are no such creatures, we continue to tell tales about them. Some of us may even find the stories more important, and the imagined creatures somehow more 'real', than any everyday occurrence. Not all such enchanted watchers claim to 'believe' that they might one day be 'beamed up' to the starship *Enterprise*, even while they act, almost, as if they do. Reminding them that *Star Trek* is 'only a story' would be wasted breath: they know very well it is a story, and yet choose to live in expectation of a humane, free-ranging Federation, in expectation (one might almost say) of the *Parousia*. It may be similarly insulting to tell more ordinary worshippers that their gods aren't 'real' – precisely because they do not think they are. Anthropologists who imagine that the peoples whom they study are *deceived* in thinking that the gods come out to dance with them on holy days (when all that 'really' happens is that the elders of the tribe, or of some other tribe, dress up as gods) are themselves unduly literal-minded. We can no more show that the gods *aren't* present by unfrocking them than we can prove that the eucharistic bread is not, after all, the body of Christ, by subjecting it to chemical analysis. Whether the rite demands a metaphorical or a metaphysical analysis instead is not to be decided quite so simply. Even without metaphysics, the rites go on, and the participants may mean nothing more by them than ritual.

Even prayer – or something that looks like prayer – is not

entirely dependent on belief in a real God. Any serious account
of what 'God' (and its cognates) means in ordinary life cannot
ignore expletives, invocations, blessings, curses. There need be
no particular common meaning in all these forms. One person's
expletive, after all, is another's phatic noise: what one means as a
literal curse another uses only as emphasis or space-filler. But
some will, in a way, be praying, even if they don't *believe* that
anyone will answer them: it is not unreasonable for those who're
drowning to call for help even in deserted places.[4] Maybe, for
some, the prayer is its own answer: not all petitions are for some
material or external good, but rather for the calm to face the
facts. Such prayers might be viewed as mantras: verbal devices
for engineering appropriate emotional or cognitive effects.
Maybe on the other hand such mantras are heard as prayers.
Clough had a point:

> Youths green and happy in first love,
> So thankful for illusion;
> And men caught out in what the world
> Calls guilt, in first confusion;
>
> And almost everyone when age,
> Disease, or sorrows strike him,
> Inclines to think there is a God,
> Or something very like him.[5]

This is not to say that these 'believe', but only that this is the
shape their minds take in such moments. This in turn is not to
say that no one at all is really 'irreligious', but only to deny that
only the literal-minded are religious. It is not necessary to plan
on being beamed up to a literal starship (though some do) to
prove oneself 'religiously sincere'. No doubt there are many who
rarely take part in public ceremonials of any kind, and recall no
sacred texts. Some of them will still make use of aphorisms or
incantations to keep up their spirits. Some of those who claim
'not to be religious' mean only that they are not members of any
particular church or sect. They may admit, or even boast, that
they do feel occasional surges of cosmic sympathy, awe-struck
appreciation, or immortal longings, but quickly add that they
don't think this any reason to amend their ways. So what is
meant by 'not being religious'? Often this may mean 'not feeling

guilty' – and the business of not feeling guilty (or affirming that no guilt is felt) may itself engender special rites of renewal. Others may admit they sometimes feel inclined to wish there was Someone they could thank, or vilify, or ask for help: wishing there were, they almost, for a moment, feel as if there is – but put the impulse on one side, as being a biologically or a culturally programmed error, to be controlled by careful recitations of the atheistical arguments. Some of the avowedly 'irreligious' are simply anti-clerical: their irreligion is their fixed determination to resist ecclesiastical authority. This too has genuinely religious roots: such personal resistance to authority makes sense only if individual persons have the right and duty to obey only their own conscience. It is also unsurprising that many such anti-clerical movements of the past succeeded only in creating a new clerisy: people who are to be respected, by all right-thinking persons, because they have particular professions. Religious forms, in short, are ones that human beings, of all beliefs and backgrounds, naturally fall into: they seek to purge themselves of improper emotions, by reliance on selected texts and rituals, and deference to persons felt to have a special tie to 'truth'.

Seeing Through Religion

But though it is true of 'religion' in general, that it need be no more than practice, this is not true of all particular 'religious' traditions. For most of the world's religious, it may be, 'disbelieving in the gods' would be like not believing in dreams, or not believing in the Bank of England. But all 'great' religions seek to transcend local observances and familiar practices. Their spokesmen profess to speak about Reality, not only about the artificial 'realities' created through ritual and recitation. They are often suspicious even of the rituals and recitations that their very own 'religion' employs to remind them of the truth. Sometimes they may reckon that 'religion' is indeed a merely human trait, to which the Gospel is opposed. This thought is not confined to the theistic religions that took their historical beginning from Abraham (though it may be no coincidence that militant atheism is a form of religious life largely confined to post-Abrahamic peoples). Buddhists too, though they are occasionally misrepresented as cheerful post-moderns, are seriously concerned for the universal truth of what they say: that there is a real escape from the realm of suffering and impermanence, not merely ways of coping with that realm: 'There is an Unborn, Unoriginated, Uncreated, Unformed. If there were not this Unborn, this Unoriginated, this Uncreated, this Unformed, escape from the world of the born, the originated, the created, the formed would not be possible.'[6]

All such seriously religious thinkers are suspicious even of 'conversion experiences' or 'sudden enlightenments' that are not fully grounded in repentance on the one hand, and rational understanding on the other. Stories, rituals, icons, offices are all the sort of thing that people will make up: the good news of the Gospel, or the Buddha's Four Noble Truths, are not 'religious' – in that ritualistic sense – since they aren't made up. We change our world by what we say of it, and change what it is we do. In thinking of the sexual act as screwing, coupling, making out or making love, the act is changed. Those who think of it as 'sacramental' (as the Song of Songs suggests) are doing something very different from those who think of it as 'fun'. By orthodox Abrahamic standards they may be in danger of idolatry.[7] Doing anything at all 'religiously' (that is, with full attention to the spirit evoked in such and such an act) may summon other spirits than the one desired. It is therefore not surprising that tradition lays down rules, for our protection in a dangerous world. If we abandoned realism in the name of a 'religion of feeling' nothing says that those feelings would not be very dark ones. As G. K. Chesterton (1874–1936) observed: 'If, in the really Dark Ages, there had been a religion of feeling, it would have been a religion of black and suicidal feeling. It was the rigid creed that resisted the rush of suicidal feeling.'[8]

Some of the religious would also challenge my earlier suggestion that art, music, story-telling, mantras, would survive the 'death of God'. Medieval paintings may be preserved in galleries, admired for their rich colouring or as links in the artistic chain. That is not what they were. Hymns are not songs, and crosses are not jewellery. Neither are prayers mere psychological devices, and those who treat them as such aren't praying:

A man that looks on glass
On it may stay his eye,
Or if he pleases, through it pass
And then the heavens espy.[9]

What matters in 'true religion' is the thing beyond: icons and sacred music can quickly become idols, fetishes and jolly tunes once we have stopped seeing *through* them. Conversely, those who have 'seen through them' may see what really matters in religion: that is to say, the Truth.

The Ethical Interpretation

For most of us, however, such asceticism is a step too far: the rituals are required to help us to remember what that truth may be, and feel its influence in our lives. But it is not therefore a truth that can only be noticed by 'religious people' or expressed only in 'religious language'. Others have argued that only those who take part in the rituals can really understand the doctrines they embody. It is indeed observably true that many who do not take part don't understand: their denial that 'God exists' bears no relation to the God addressed in worship. The philosopher George Berkeley (1685–1753) came close to saying that moral and religious utterances were just devices for awakening appropriate emotions – as it might be, 'love, hope, gratitude, and obedience...agreeably to that notion of saving faith which is required in a Christian'.[10] Accordingly, to *believe* the doctrine is to act as God would wish, even if there were no God, or even if we could not, in the abstract, say what God would do:

> May not Christians...be allowed to believe the divinity of our Saviour, or that in Him God and man make one Person, and be verily persuaded thereof, so far as for such faith or belief to become a real principle of life and conduct? inasmuch as, by virtue of such persuasion, they submit to His government, believe His doctrine, and practise His precepts, although they form no abstract idea of the union between the divine and human nature; nor may be able to clear up the notion of *person* to the contentment of a minute philosopher.[11]

There is, after all, no universally agreed account of what a *human* person is: it does not follow that we cannot recognize one, or deal well by her. It isn't absurd to suggest that 'being a person' is simply, for practical purposes, being someone whom the speaker urges us to respect. On this account, perhaps, to say that Christ is King is only to commit ourselves to living in love and charity with our neighbour, while encouraging ourselves in this by fantasy and verbal music. We can certainly agree with Berkeley that 'the faith of a true Christian must be a lively faith that sanctifies the heart and shews itself in the fruits of the Spirit':[12]

> Religion is no such speculative knowledge which rests merely in the understanding. She makes her residence in the heart, warms the affections and engages the will.[13] ... A Man may frame the most accurate Notions, and in one Sense attain the exactest Knowledge of God and Christ that human Faculties can reach, and yet, notwithstanding all this, be far from knowing them in that saving Sense.... To know God as we ought, we must love him; and love him so as withal to love our Brethren, his Creatures and his Children.[14]

We can also agree that much religious utterance is difficult or impossible to translate into less 'musical' form. 'The Apostle himself, who was caught up into the 3rd heaven, could give us no other than this empty tho emphatical description of it. 'tis wt eye hath not seen nor ear heard neither hath it enter'd into the heart of man to conceive.'[15] We can even agree that most attempts at theological analysis will be futile or divisive:

> The Christian religion was calculated for the Bulk of Mankind, and therefore cannot reasonably be supposed to consist in subtle and nice notions.... The making of Religion a notional Thing, hath been of infinite Disservice. And whereas its holy Mysteries are rather to be received with Humility of Faith, than defined and measured by the Accuracy of human Reason; all Attempts of this Kind, however well intended, have visibly failed in the Event; and instead of reconciling Infidels, have by creating Disputes and Heats among the Professors of Christianity, given no small Advantage to its Enemies.[16]

But Berkeley did not therefore contend that such doctrines have no 'assertoric' significance: indeed he devoted his energies to showing that theism was a more rational view of things than atheism, and that there was more to hope for than *this* life provided.[17] Even if full understanding demands action – both ethical and ritual – we may still understand, in part, what the doctrine that demands the action is.

Identifying This and That

My distinction between 'the great religions' and 'religion in general' is neither absolute nor all-important. The religiously inclined of any age may try to speak of Something that is not contained in any human description, even theirs. Shamans may seriously believe, as much as modern scientists, that they have access to a real world, a causally important world, beyond the human. They may be confident that people in another age or tribe could as easily, and maybe do, have access to that same Real World, even if they use other words and images. When the Greeks identified Egyptian gods with the Olympians they were expressing their conviction that Olympians were *real*, and variously described in different cultures: it would be, at best, a manner of speaking to suggest that (for example) Judge Dee was the Chinese Sherlock Holmes. It might be literally true that Ammon-Ra was Zeus: not 'the Egyptian Zeus' but Zeus Himself as He was perceived and talked about in Egypt. Holmes and Dee are limited (as fictional entities) by the stories told of them in a way that, maybe, Zeus and Ammon-Ra, Isis and Athena, aren't. Much the same things must be said of Dee and Holmes if it is to make sense to equate them, but 'real beings' may be described quite differently by different people and yet be the same.

Apuleius spoke, we may suppose, for his own beliefs when he wrote of how the Goddess showed herself to a repentant and despairing Lucius (transformed into an ass and longing for his restoration): 'my single godhead is adored by the whole world in varied forms, in differing rites and with many diverse names', she says, going on to identify herself as Pessinuntia, Minerva, Venus, Diana, Proserpine, Ceres, Juno, Bellona, Hecate, Rhamnusia, and 'under her true name' as Queen Isis.[18]

But though there may have been those who fully 'believed' Olympian religion, or 'Isisism', there were also others who thought it only a grand metaphor for human life, and others who did not think at all, but still kept ritual observances. They sought to live as mortals, under the eye of gods, even if the question of the gods' 'existence' could not easily be settled. Maybe that is also true for many nowadays. If it were established that theistic (or Buddhistic) claims are false, 'religion' would not vanish from the world. But the 'great religions', in their greatness – a class that may once have included Isis-worship and Olympian religion – would. Those who deny that we can ever transcend the limits of our place and time can only serve a local deity, which 'exists' only in the hearts and minds of its people. They cannot look beyond the glass – and therefore only see themselves. It is, perhaps, significant that religious practices are now so often defended as 'traditional', as being important to a family's, or a nation's, sense of being. Missionary zeal is frowned on, as converts lose their natural home to be inducted into an 'alien faith'. Syncretic movements, granting a place to every nation's heritage, are more allowable than would be possible if any particular faith claimed 'real truth'.

Might it be true instead that (say) the Olympian gods together constitute a range of human possibilities that would be familiar in all tribes and ages, and yet have no real being outside the human heart? Maybe whenever people tell their stories some figure like Zeus will turn up in them, and in the world where people live: people attempt to achieve a Zeus-like character and status, and what they do becomes, in turn, a story. According to William Blake, 'the characters of Chaucer's Pilgrims are the characters which compose all ages and nations'.[19] And again: 'visions of these eternal principles or characters of human life appear to poets, in all ages: the Grecian gods were the ancient Cherubim of Phoenicia... These gods are visions of the eternal attributes, or divine names'.[20] But it is just as likely that such story-gods, like other characters, have their being only in some very specific settings. The Greeks were wrong to think of Ammon-Ra as Zeus-like, just as they would be wrong to expect all human beings, of whatever time or place, to cultivate exactly those virtues that 'the Greeks' approved. The similarity of human character is not enough to guarantee so great a similarity of imagined excellence. The 'great religions' tell us what we don't already know (or do not know we know): religions that are only expressions of human character and interest are likely to be as different as human character and interest can make them. Van Gulik's Judge Dee (a married magistrate with strong Confucian views and a quick temper) is *not* the same as Conan Doyle's Holmes (a bachelor of partly rationalist temperament, and a very low boredom threshold). The Plowman of Chaucer is not, *pace* Blake, 'Hercules in his supreme eternal state'.

Such relativism or syncretism seems at first more tolerant than realism. But there is no good reason to suppose that local, fictional deities are more humane. The idea that 'relativism' is kindlier or more liberal than 'absolutism' is simply silly: on the contrary, anyone who thinks that there is a 'fact of the matter', independent of her own fond belief or feeling, is thereby admitting that she might be wrong; those who deny that there is any truth are free to infer that they are *never* wrong, and insist on doing things *their* way. Even syncretists, in practice, can be quite intolerant: inevitably so, since their demand must be that no one think she's *right*. When King Belshazzar put all the sacred vessels of the peoples Babylon had conquered on display, he probably did not intend to praise them, even if he expected that their worshippers would find a place of some sort in the wider cult. When Babylon fell it gave the people of Israel a lasting metaphor for the collapse of all such grandiose schemes. Empires do not want their subjects to believe that there is any Outside: they may allow local or tribal or professional cults, but only on condition that 'the peace' is not disturbed, and that no one treats their god as anything more than a fetish or good-luck charm. Syncretism and atheism are close allies.

The Noble Truths of Theism

My topic is that real Outside: the truth professed in theism. Not every theist has been an Abrahamist: many instead have taken inspiration from the Greek, and chiefly the Platonic, tradition (which has also influenced the development of more ordinarily Abrahamist faiths). There are also recognizable theists of African and Hindu extraction, whose arguments – were this a global survey – should certainly be considered. Much of my own system owes as much to Plato as to Abraham – why then do I chiefly speak of 'Abrahamic religions', and what do I mean?

I certainly do not intend to suggest that 'Judaism', 'Christianity' and 'Islam' – the three chief inheritors of Abraham's vision – should be conceived as bearers of a putative 'Judaeo-Christo-Islamic' tradition, or that what they share is necessarily what is most important to each of them. But it is equally true that 'Buddhist' sects are very various: all acknowledge their historical connection to Gautama Buddha, but have each their own scriptures, teachings and ceremonials. It is still possible to speak of certain central themes that all acknowledge:[21] so also with the many peoples whose founding legend mentions Abraham. 'The Lord said to Abram, "Leave your own country, your kinsmen, and your father's house, and go to a country that I will show you"' (Genesis 12.1). That recurrent theme, of departure and rejection of all former household gods, lies at the root of every branch of Abraham's inheritors. Whereas Greek (and Hindu) theists are ready to accept the ancient gods as images, or fragments, of the One True God (so that the last great Greek philosopher, Plotinus, allegorized obscure Homeric myths as expressing philosophically discovered truths), Abrahamists are likelier to suspect that the gods of the nations are but idols.

Despite that difference, most theists would insist that there is and can be only One True God, and that Abraham, Moses, Isaiah, Plato, Cleanthes, Jesus, Plotinus, Mohammad, Aquinas, Baha'ullah and Ramanujah all address that God. It's not that there are many different candidates for being God: theism is a way of talking about That Than Which None Greater Can Be Conceived, and the allegiance of such theists must always be to that One God, not to their image of that God. That is what makes them theists, of the great tradition, rather than devotees of local godlings which gain their power only from that devotion. It certainly makes sense to say that the gods of one age may be the fairies, or the comic characters of another: people no longer take the stories seriously, and mock their ancestors' cult-practices as readily as they mock their dress-sense. But this is just to say that none of those gods was God. God as any of us conceives Him is not the same as God – even if we have no choice but to revere Him under the guise of our own best conception.

Even as a literary character, of course, there is good reason to insist that 'God' is one, even if many different writers had a hand in His depiction. Some literary characters – especially those that feature in early epics – have survived their authors, so that 'Odysseus' now means more than Homer's cunning Greek. Not every attempt to tell a story of Odysseus will be included in the canon, any more than every story that purports to be about God. Different critics may praise different canons, but it is not unreasonable to think that Torah, Bible and Koran do feature 'the same figure'. But as a literary character 'God' – even the God of Torah, Bible and Koran – is not God: as St Anselm (1033–1109) put it, a being that exists only *in intellectu* is inferior to one that exists *in intellectu* and also *in re*: in fact as well as in fancy. A merely fanciful God, existing only by the magic of our words, is not the God and Creator, any more than any other idol. If fictional gods are all the gods there are, there is no God.

So what is it that theists say about that One True God, and why might it be true? What follows is a deliberately dry account. Anyone who really follows it may discover that the argument itself is a 'religious' one, a way of recalling jaded spirits. But it is intended as an argument – or set of arguments – that anyone could follow, and even accept, without any wish to join in ritual observances – except perhaps in prayer. Even those who do not accept it may at least understand theism better: some traditional believers, and some militant atheists, conspire to insist that the God of the Philosophers is not the God of Abraham. No one, they say, can really be 'religious' who doubts the simple, 'literal' application of anthropomorphic stories about God, or dislikes ceremonial. I shall contend, on the contrary, that the theses of philosophical theism are embedded in Jewish, Christian and Islamic tradition: those who worship any other god, or God under any other description than that endorsed by orthodox philosophical theologians, are – traditionally – heretics or even idolaters. It is heretical, in every major Abrahamic tradition, to suppose that 'God' names one imaginable 'bigger' being amongst many. 'God' has never named an Old Man in the Sky. Even the authors of *Star Trek* know better: whenever the crew encounter some powerful entity proclaiming itself to be 'God', they respond that nothing less than the Omnipotent, Omniscient, Omnipresent can merit worship. Realist, and believing, theologians have always insisted that God does not *exist*, does not stand out from an independent background as a bigger, louder creature – and yet is real. 'God does not belong to the class of existing things: not that he has no existence, but that he is above all existing things, nay even above existence itself.'[22] 'Any existing God would be less than God. An existent God would be an idol or a demon.'[23]

One way of interpreting a claim like that would be to say that 'God' names whatever is supremely worshipful: not what *is* but what *ought* to be. This too can be understood in at least two ways: either what *ought* to be is merely what 'we' insist upon (and 'God' is only a human figment) or else the very fact of *being obligatory* is, exactly, the supreme fact, which explains why lesser things are as they are. God, as conceived by the tradition, is first encountered in the context of a moral and political demand: to leave a corrupt society, and make a new one. That God, so conceived, is the true creator and owner of all other things, is a claim about the vindication of morality. Theists do not first imagine that an unknown entity created everything, and thence infer what actions It requires of us (though even this is not an altogether foolish method). They rather insist that, despite appearances, the Just will triumph. This is one reason why, if it were to emerge that, after all, the Lord did *not* make the heavens, it would still be possible to worship the Lord. Or rather it would be possible initially: there are more difficulties than atheistical commentators, or post-modernists, suppose in conceiving a truly godless universe in which it would still be reasonable to prefer one outcome to another (but that is by the way). That 'moral' argument I shall address in later chapters.

So what are the rules of Abrahamic orthopraxis? The demand of true, theistical religion of the Abrahamic kind – whether the claim is interpreted by realists or anti-realists – is to do justice and love mercy. The Ten Commandments (popularly so called) define a form of society. Do not steal, or seek to kill; do not cause marital troubles; do not envy others; do not claim that God requires what God does not; do not always treat everything as if it were a tool or stuff for your own purposes (allow all things their space); do not betray your neighbour; honour those from whom you gained your life. Above all, never let another ideal or goal take precedence over those divine requirements. In brief, let nothing matter more to you than leaving everything its space: remember, you were slaves in Egypt. Atheistical commentators, or spokesmen of the Secular Society (and other similarly nineteenth-century hold-outs), will often complain about the 'absolutist' or 'authoritarian' or 'joyless' character of the Commandments. It may be true that some who have obeyed the commandments have been 'joyless': it is hard to see why disobeying them would have been much better. Of course we are often tempted to disobey them: that is why it's worth recalling them.

Consider for example the command to 'keep the sabbath'. No doubt this has – against both spirit and letter of the law – been used to excuse backbiting, or neglect of duty. In origins the sabbath was an occasion when we were not to *use* the world: not to gather food, or fuel, nor yet to require that servants gather food or fuel, in ways that interfered with the lives of others. It was not only the seventh day that was set aside: on the seventh day of every week, in the seventh year and in the fiftieth the land was to be left for the poor, and the wild things of the country (Leviticus 25. 6–10). The prophet Amos (8.5) linked the sabbath, explicitly, to bans on the commercial exploitation of the poor. The duty of contemplation carries social consequences. Treating the land, and those we share it with, as mere material is forbidden, and our disobedience will have its results. The sabbatarian principle requires that all those loyal to the Covenant set time aside to recognize the fact that the world and the creatures in it aren't entirely 'ours'.[24]

When Babylon has fallen, 'there no Arab shall pitch his tent, no shepherds fold their flocks. There marmots shall have their lairs, and porcupines shall overrun her houses; there desert owls shall dwell, and there he-goats shall gambol' (Isaiah 13.20f). 'The whole world has rest and is at peace; it breaks into cries of joy. The pines themselves and the cedars of Lebanon exult over you: since you have been laid low, they say, no man comes up to fell us' (Isaiah 14.7f). The land shall have the sabbaths we denied to it (Leviticus 26.34). If we want a share in the sabbath, we must not seek to deny it to others. As I remarked some years ago:

The natural historian of a future age may be able to point to the particular follies that brought ruin – chopping down the tropical rain forests, meditating nuclear war, introducing hybrid monocultures, spreading poisons, financing grain-mountains, and rearing cattle in conditions that clearly breach the spirit of the commandment not to muzzle the ox that treads out the corn (Deuteronomy 25.4). The historian whose eyes are opened to the acts of God will have no doubt we brought our ruin on ourselves, that it is God's answer to the arrogant.[25]

When I speak of *God*, the connotations should not be forgotten. It is still possible to begin, for purposes of argument, with metaphysics, even if that was not quite the route the first believers took. In fact, it is necessary for us to begin with metaphysics, since the status of ethics is itself in dispute. Theologians, even believing theologians, have of late been persuaded that they *must* adopt a merely 'ethical' account of God, or even a fully anti-realist account, because (so they have been led to believe) the claims of metaphysical theism have been disproved, or made to seem ridiculous. Such theologians usually gesture towards Kant's supposed dissection of the standard arguments, on the one hand, and towards the successes of a secular science on the other. This is, or so I myself believe, an error, founded – most often – in a misunderstood empiricism on the one hand, and the exaggerated claims of scientific materialism on the other.[26] It is high time that Kantian arguments were put to rest, and the successes of 'science' seen for what they are – evidence for the real existence of God (*aka*, the friendliness of Being).

TWO

PHILOSOPHY AND THE BETRAYAL OF THOUGHT

Misunderstanding the Enlightenment

WESTERN THEOLOGIANS HAVE been convinced too easily that post-Kantian philosophy has made traditional theology impossible. Some think that 'philosophy', or Enlightenment philosophy, gives human reason too much scope: revelation or inspiration or imagination matter more than reason. Others think that philosophers themselves have shown that reason cannot reach beyond the world, and thence deduce either that 'religion' must be this-worldly or (again) that it must rest in faculties beyond philosophy. Anti-realists and anti-rationalists alike condemn 'natural theology'. So even before I argue, philosophically, for the truths of theism, I must make it plausible that philosophical discourse is not essentially godless.

It is certainly true that all too many students issue from undergraduate philosophy courses immunized against enthusiasm, in the conceit that they have answers to all the old conundrums, which were (they suppose) no more than verbal trickery. Plenty of philosophers really mind about the truth, and want to be Socratic in pursuit of it: Socrates' sceptical attack was spring-cleaning, and the first step towards uncovering knowledge. But the danger of stumbling at that step is real. If all that matters is debunking past philosophers, how does that differ from repeated refutation of the Chaldaean Oracles or the Prophecies of Nostradamus? Theologians who don't reckon themselves prophets may be tempted to align themselves with creative writers, or even literary critics, rather than to challenge the debunkers, or accept their verdict. This is, I suggest, an error. What was the real intent of the Enlightenment philosophers, and what did they achieve?

René Descartes is depicted, in those undergraduate courses, as the Father of Modern Philosophy – and a failure. Seeking to secure himself against the errors of sense and of scholasticism, he found a sure foundation in the realization, shared by Augustine (and even a character in one of Plautus' plays),[1] that he was certainly thinking even when he raised a doubt about that truth, and that therefore someone existed to think that thought. From that uttermost limit of Cartesian scepticism he devised a way of proving God's existence, and hence the general reliability of his senses, when they were treated with a cautious respect. Students are taught that even the *cogito*[2] is unreliable: granted there is a thought (as it might be: 'perhaps there are no substances at all')[3], but why assume that thoughts must have a thinker? Even if that much is granted, how should we advance from a supposedly clear notion of a perfect being to the actual existence of such a thing? Existence, we learn, is not a predicate, and nothing has a nature such that it must exist *in re*. And even if there were a perfect being, what is to prove that it must speak the truth (unless we already know, or 'clearly conceive', that perfect beings do)?

It would seem to follow that modern analysis leaves us worse off than Descartes. Apparently we are not justified in thinking that we really exist, or that an external or material world exists. None of those theses can be established beyond doubt. We might indeed ('might logically') be the victims of mad scientists or extraterrestrial intelligence. If I *knew* that I was typing this on my personal computer, I would *know* whatever I saw followed logically from that known fact: as it might be, I *know* that there are no advanced and mischievous intelligences in the universe who love to deceive inhabitants of lesser planets, no Googols,[4] who are deceiving me in this. But as I plainly do *not* know such a thing (for I know far too little about how often life, intelligence and trickery appear), I do not know even what is most obvious to me. If p, then q: not-q, so not-p. If I knew anything, I would know that no Googols existed to deceive me on that point; I do not, so I know nothing on which they could deceive me. Nor, by parity of argument, do I even 'justifiably believe' any such thing. The only honourable conclusion would seem to be to scepticism of a more than Cartesian kind.

The argument may seem self-refuting: after all, one other thing I do not know is that this argument is valid. But if I don't know that, it does not follow (or I do not see its following) that I have after all sound reasons for my beliefs. Maybe the hidden premise, that knowledge (and justifiable belief) is transitive, is false: maybe I can know p, but not therefore know any of the things that I can see do logically follow from that p. This is the move preferred by Nozick,[5] but it seems to be as sceptical in its import as the first and swift surrender. If I don't know even what 'follows logically' from a 'known' truth, I hardly know what such a known truth means, nor what it means to know it: the very notion of 'sound reasoning' collapses. 'Therefore the wise man will suspend judgement about everything'.[6]

Students are taught to evade, as they suppose, such Pyrrhonism (named after Pyrrho of Elis, who gave no assent to anything, and so was not disturbed by anything), by remembering that the Cartesian strategy is not for every day. No one, we insist, can really question the normal, waking world, and draw herself back into the lonely *cogito*. Indeed, we could not even express that *cogito*: self-identification, and the thought that there's a thought expressed, both need the context of a public universe and a public language. To the question, 'Am I dreaming?', the answer must be 'No'. No one – or no one who is anyone – seriously doubts her own, and material, reality. But this too is sceptical in its import. If truth is one thing and our words another, there is always a real possibility of error. If we can sometimes truly judge that we were wrong, it must remain an open possibility that we will soon be judging so again – about our present dogmas. The only way of closing off that thought is to insist that we can manage well-enough with what we take to be present agreement, that the limits of our language are the limits of our world. 'Truth', or the only truth that we could mind about, is 'what it is better for us to believe, rather than the accurate representation of reality'.[7] That concept 'better', of course, does not mean 'really better', but rather 'what we choose to think is better'. That concept 'we' means only what the speaker and her audience wish it to. Descartes, like other great philosophers, thought it possible that we might discover Truth:[8] present-day critics of his enterprise apparently insist that the Truth we could be wrong about is one we can't discover. To be 'wrong' in the only important sense is simply to be out of step with our contemporaries (so someone or other says). Pyrrhonists are typically conservatives: granted that neither side in any dispute can establish itself as *right*, it's always easier to 'go with the flow'. If the limits of language are the limits of our world, there is no escape from tyranny: 'the purpose of Newspeak was not only to provide a medium of expression for the world-view and mental habits proper to the devotees of Ingsoc, but to make all other modes of thought impossible'.[9] If there is no real Outside that we could reach, then the whole distinction between 'the human world' and 'the real world' is null.

This is to accept the popular conclusion of Kant's arguments. Kant claimed that earlier philosophers had hoped to demonstrate real truths about the real world, existing independently of anything we thought or did. By showing (so he said) that contradictory conclusions followed when they sought to use our common concepts to describe that 'real world', he seemed to show that we could not know anything about it: our knowledge, so to call it, must be restricted to the world whose structure we dictated. We could only 'know' the world as we experienced it, and must therefore – so his successors said – content ourselves with merely 'human' truths. The Truth Itself must be inscrutable, and therefore there was no use for such a concept. Kant himself was not so sceptical: there was, as I shall argue, a route through doubt to moral certainty for him as for his predecessors. But the effect (except for those who firmly said that we could after all expect to know more than we did about 'things in themselves') was to make Truth a grand unknown.

The result, which may be very far from any academic's hope, may well be to assure our students that they had better choose to conform, but not of course to assent, to fashionable thought in their own stratum of society. So they bind themselves, as good Pyrrhonian sceptics, to the quadruple compulsion of Nature, desire, custom and the rules of such crafts as they elect to practise, so as not to be wholly inactive.[10] This indolent agreement is so much in accord with fashionable dictats on the dangers of enthusiasm, and smug 'deconstructions' of other people's certainties, as to be well-rewarded. It is also recognizable, at least to those who have sometimes escaped it, as a mild form of depression. 'Obviously' ordinary usage rules: or rather, what we judge 'ordinary' for our time and place, here at the tail end of twentieth-century progress, is self-evidently 'true'. Not even the strange theories of high physicists have much effect: they make for splendid stories, but we don't *believe* them, even if we say that they are true. Either there is no truth beyond the ordinarily obvious, or it is humanly inconceivable (and so irrelevant).

Return to Rational Realism

Self-consciously 'post-modern' thinkers who have despaired of Truth are only one sect amongst many. There are still 'modernists' amongst us, firmly convinced that decent history began in 1859, or 1945, or some time last year. But modernists like that are the best reason to be post-modern. As Chesterton put it:

> The whole object of history is to make us realize that humanity can be great and glorious, under conditions quite different and even contrary to our own.... If you cannot see Man, divine and democratic, under the disguises of all the centuries, why on earth should you suppose you will be able to see him under the disguises of all the nations and tribes? If the Dark Ages must be as dark as they look, why are the black men not as black as they are painted? If I may feel supercilious towards a Chaldaean, why not towards a Chinaman? If I may despise a Roman for not having a steam-plough, why not a Russian for not wanting a steam-plough? If scientific industry [or any other fashionable nostrum] is the supreme historical test, it divides us as much from backward peoples as from bygone peoples. It divides even European peoples from each other.[11]

This is not to say that other times and places are correct because they say they are: on the contrary, it is because there is a real world, larger than any single human vision, that we can and should respect those alien insights. Chesterton's praise of reason, and objective truth, is the centre of his whole philosophy. The means whereby Father Brown detects the great thief Flambeau (disguised as a priest) in the earliest and one of the best Brown stories, you may recall, is that Flambeau 'attacked reason: it's bad theology':[12]

Reason and justice grip the remotest and the loneliest star.

Look at those stars. Don't they look as if they were single diamonds and sapphires? Well, you can imagine any mad botany or geology you please. Think of forests of adamant with leaves of brilliants. Think the moon is a blue moon, a single elephantine sapphire. But don't fancy that all that frantic astronomy would make the smallest difference to the reason and justice of conduct. On plains of opal, under cliffs cut out of pearl, you would still find a notice-board: 'Thou shalt not steal.'

The filmed version, ludicrously enough, had Flambeau betraying himself by eating ham on Friday. Chesterton was well aware that much of Europe, over many centuries, was quite dark (and perhaps that film confirms his point). But it was (and is) only dark in patches, lit by long, narrow rays like searchlights:

And just as any man, however much in darkness, if he looks right down the searchlight, looks into a furnace of white-hot radiance, so any medieval man, who had the luck to hear the right lectures or look at the right manuscript, did not merely 'follow a gleam', a grey glimmer in a mystical forest; but looked straight down the ages into the radiant mind of Aristotle.... Such light as they had came, not only from the broad daylight, but from the brilliant daylight; it was the buried sunlight of the Mediterranean.[13]

The same can be true today.

In outlining Aquinas's thought – in what Étienne Gilson said, with some justice, was the best book ever written on Aquinas[14] – Chesterton chose to emphasize its rational realism. The fundamental truths of reason are that 'there is an Is':[15] the brute fact of existence. The recognition of that Being carries with it the understanding that contradictories cannot both be true, that propositions of the form 'p & not-p' are impossible. By these ladders of logic 'St. Thomas besieged and mounted the House of Man,...climbed up the turrets and talked with angels on the roofs of gold'.[16]

It is fashionable to say that there is no Truth, or that we cannot find it out, or that the laws of non-contradiction and excluded middle have been (simultaneously) disproved by physicists and revealed as bourgeois or masculinist plots. There are some insights to be gained even from these apparent follies: but even such insights can't be gained by anyone but rational realists. It is even fashionable to adopt Siger of Brabant's Two Truth theory, that the provinces of scientific knowledge and religion are so far distinct that what is false in science may be true – or sort-of-true – in religion. It was this, by Chesterton's account, that roused Aquinas to a last great burst of fury.[17] As a rational realist, even if not a Thomist, I applaud Aquinas's and Chesterton's intransigence in this. 'Religion's passionate interest' – and philosophy's – 'is in a truth which is not merely something posited by its own passion and actual only in that passion, but in a truth which is independent of it and prior to it.'[18] 'Truisms are true, hold on to that! The solid world exists, its laws do not change'.[19] There can be no argument with those who choose to deny this – for argument and even assertion depend on there being real truths and real laws of logic. It is enough, perhaps, to say that every attempt to utter Ingsoc's creed – the creed of anti-realists – requires so much doublethink as to corrupt both language and the soul. At the heart of every sane discussion lies a wordless recognition of mere fact, the realization that we are not God. Those who say there is no Truth are liars; those who say we cannot find it out admit they have no reason for what they say. 'We must both say and think that Being Is.' That will be the topic of the following chapter.

The Metaphysics of Morals

Kant himself suggested that we must recognize the demands of duty, and could thence conclude that we were 'really' free although it looked to us, being bound to conceive the world like this, as if our motions were determined by physical circumstance. In saying so Kant stood in a great tradition: unfortunately, what too many thought they learned from him was simply that any objective duty must conflict with the will's freedom. Moral judgement, they concluded, must be an individual's business: to believe that anything but one's own will dictated what one should do was to be, pejoratively, 'heteronomous'. Not only God, but any moral order, must therefore be abjured, as being 'immoral'. How this claim can ever avoid self-contradiction is not my concern.

Other writings in the great tradition have contributed to this strange doctrine: the doctrine, that is, that moral judgement is never right or wrong, but only sincere or insincere (strangely, being insincere or hypocritical is wrong, though nothing else is). Even George Berkeley, for example, thought that 'moral and religious utterances' had an *emotive*, not an assertoric meaning. 'Truth. 3 sorts thereof Natural, Mathematical & Moral.'[20] Of those three sorts, only the 'natural' involves 'what is the case' (as it might be, 'There are children playing in the street outside'). Mathematical truths, he there suggests (mistakenly), are functions only of the words we use. 'Moral truths', so called, are measured by 'the general good of mankind', and 'believed' simply in being acted on. But Berkeley's distinction is not quite so clear. Words in general do not 'mean' by standing for or exciting clear and distinct ideas: sometimes they are no more than place-holders, or expressions of a lively hope for something more. We understand a sentence when we know what can be done with it: moral utterances are not so different from 'natural' ones. In fact our understanding of what is the case amounts, for Berkeley, to knowing what God wishes us to do: correct description of the natural world is to engage in conversation with the God who guides us – but that is another story.

The emotive interpretation of moral, and religious, utterance still has its effects. It is widely believed that there is an error, called 'the naturalistic fallacy', which amounts to thinking that any moral judgement is correct in virtue of the way things are. To say that (say) children should not be beaten can only be to forbid their being beaten: the prohibition cannot rest in any true account of children, or of being beaten. The argument, such as it is, for this is as follows. Either we define 'children' as 'creatures who should not be beaten' or simply as 'young members of our species'. If we do the former then the claim that they should not be beaten lacks any substantive sense, being only a tautology. If we do the latter then the claim that they should not be beaten is a claim – so critics say – about their natural properties which cannot be tested: other claims about children (that they are less than four feet tall, have high voices and short attention spans) are generalizations to which we might find exceptions (or at least know what exceptions there might be). That children are creatures who are not to be beaten is not of this order, as though we could discover a sub-set of children who, unusually, *should* be, though they differ in no other significant respect. Any reason that we offer to believe that they are not to be beaten must suffer the same flaw. We can't even usefully suggest that children are creatures who *strike* us as not to be beaten: that might be true, but gives us no good reason not to beat them (after all, they strike some people as creatures to be fondled – or to be beaten). Accordingly the claim, being neither a tautology nor yet an empirical generalization, cannot be truly assertoric.

If the same analysis is made for religious utterances (as 'God is to be worshipped') these too must have some other function than the assertoric. It may seem that religious texts are full of statements: but the statements will not be 'religious', and the truly religious utterances will really be commands, or pleas, or mere ejaculations. No such things are ever 'true' or 'false' – and none can ever have true reasons: being a reason for action, on this account, is not the sort of thing that can be true, but only (roughly) acceptable. We accept (that is we here accept) the status of children as 'not to be beaten', but for no good reason. Equally, we accept (or not) the status of the world as 'to be prayed for', or of certain scriptures as 'to be read'. Religion must be something that we do, not something we believe, because it contains no statements to believe or not.

But G. E. Moore (1873–1958), who popularized this sort of argument, had quite different intentions. In denying that 'good' could mean the same as 'socially approved' or 'helpful to humanity' or 'pleasant', he relied upon a firm, and Platonist, intuition: that we could reasonably *ask* whether what was socially approved (or whatever else) was *good*. All such substantive judgements were true, or not, in consequence of real relations, not of what we said. He relied, that is, on brute recognition of a real thing, namely 'goodness'. So far from saying that none of our moral judgements ever could have reasons, or be true, he insisted that there was a fact of the matter, whether this or that were good, which we could only hope to realize (however fallibly) by reason. Just as we decide what counts as true by finding what we can consistently rely on, so we find out what is good by working out what reasonable priorities we have. It is certainly *possible* that we are wrong: it may be, for example, that human life is not after all a good, although we can hardly ourselves think otherwise, and could not count on any wide agreement, amongst humans, that it wasn't. The very fact that we could, in fact, be wrong, even in our most serious and well-considered judgements, is evidence (as Moore supposed) that there were real moral facts. Indeed the supreme moral fact was just what it was for Plato: the Good Itself requires our attention. Certainly we cannot demonstrate that (say) human life is, on the whole, a good, any more than we can demonstrate that Googols don't exist. In ethics and in science alike we must rely on faith, on indemonstrable axioms.

The Reach of Reason

Other authors of the texts we study have also been misjudged. It is commonly assumed that philosophy since the Enlightenment has been profoundly 'secular' in inspiration, and atheistical in outcome. But there were very few such atheistical philosophers, and the arguments they offered were usually not meant to have the effects they did. Nor indeed should they have had. There is less danger than some theologians have supposed in studying philosophy.

It does not follow that philosophy is all that matters. There are truths (who can deny it?) that we do not know, and cannot even sketch. In Berkeley's words: 'Methinks it may consist with all due deference to the greatest of human understandings, to suppose them ignorant of many things, which are not suited to their faculties, or lie out of their reach.'[21] We can properly believe what we don't understand, because it would be insane to think that what *we* cannot understand cannot express a truth.[22] A religion wholly 'reasonable' in containing nothing that we could not 'understand' (could not form representative ideas of) would have less force. We may not know *why* something happens as it does, nor *why* it would be best to behave (say) as the scriptures say: it does not follow that it would be sensible to choose a different path. Maybe the wise can afford to act only on their own best understandings: we aren't wise. 'It may be owned that the Gentiles might by a due use of their reason, by thought and study, observing the beauty and order of the world, and the excellency and profitableness of virtue, have obtained some sense of a Providence and of Religion . . . But how few were they who made this use of their reason, or lived according to it.'[23]

Descartes, Berkeley, Kant and many others have been interpreted as showing how difficult it is to defend quite ordinary beliefs. We can have no idea of anything that transcends our experience – and therefore have no idea of substance, identity, causation, decency, or God. Or rather the only ideas of this sort we can have will be ones we can equate with ordinary perceptions: A's being caused by B can only be A's regularly following B in a way that is itself followed by an expectation of seeing A when we have seen B; A's being the very same thing as B can only be our happening to count 'them' both together. Strangely, the very people who think themselves most 'empirical' are also those who talk about distant galaxies, or the first three seconds of the universe – matters which plainly far transcend any possible experience of ours. David Hume's analysis of human knowledge eliminates most scientific theory in the process of eliminating theological realism. Such realism, some say, 'can only actually be true for a heteronomous consciousness such as no normal person ought now to have'.[24] That claim, it is my contention, is absurd: it rests, in fact, on a misreading of the philosophical tradition. The Death of God (reputed) has been followed by the death of reason, science and self.

The triumph of an unacknowledged Pyrrhonism has turned on the supposed failure of some philosophers to establish truth-in-fact for their hypotheses, and on the supposedly firm arguments of others for the impossibility of our uncovering Truth. All that we can hope for, it is thought, is an *agreement* – and this is easier, so it is thought, for theses about plain matters of fact than for moral or religious ones. In agreeing to speak of plain, material objects (even though we have no guarantee of their existence), and to differ about our moral or religious values, we have, without acknowledging it, voted against theism. We haven't *discovered* that there is no real, objective order, but decided not to pay attention to it, lest we be found in the wrong. We have panicked at the thought of what the world, the real world, might be, and chosen to stay sleeping – while simultaneously claiming that this choice is a rational, 'enlightened' one. Rorty's claim embodies the same confusion: 'such thoughts may be hard to live with, Rorty implies, *but live with them we must*.[25] If there is anything we 'must' live with, then not everything is subject to our redescriptions. Quite a lot of things, indeed, aren't quite so easy to eliminate: some things simply cannot be magicked away. If anti-realism is correct 'what is to stop us eliminating death, poverty and unhappiness by conceptual revisions?'[26] Does it seem improbable that we would try? Cupitt does:

> I don't accept the view...that there are a lot of pre-cultural and purely objective, but very unpleasant, facts about the human condition, which are non-narrative and just the same for every human being. On the contrary, sickness, old age, suffering, death, transience and futility are construed in very different ways in different religions and philosophies....We can make old age venerable or pitiful. We can make death either the crown of life and the achievement of the highest social status, or we can make it an outrage. The choice is ours.[27]

The threat is a real one. After all, there is precedent for it:

> Hail horrours, hail
> Infernal world, and thou profoundest Hell
> Receive thy new Possessor: One who brings
> A mind not to be changed by Place or Time.
> The mind is its own place, and in itself
> Can make a Heav'n of Hell, a Hell of Heav'n.[28]

By selecting different words for what others might call a victim, we are free of blame: call the thing a neonate, an embryo, a pre-embryo; call it an oncomouse, an animal preparation or a walking larder. Those particular evasions are aided by a curious piece of doublethink:[29] the preferred expressions are chosen as being devoid of any moral force of a contentious kind, but then employed to justify what would have been contentious morals. First we insist that the moral question must not be begged, and so rule out such words as 'murder' in favour of 'homicide' or 'termination'; then we infer that since the act, so described, lacked any moral import, we may properly perform it. If things are only and entirely what 'we' call them, argument becomes irrefutable, and hence impossible. If everything is what we choose to call it, we can call anything 'reason' (but why bother). As Orwell put it:

> Has it ever occurred to you, Winston, that by the year 2050, at the very latest, not a single human being will be alive who could understand such a conversation as we are having now?' 'Except – –' began Winston doubtfully, and then stopped. It had been on the tip of his tongue to say 'Except the proles', but he checked himself, not feeling fully certain that this remark was not in some way unorthodox. Syme, however had divined what he was about to say. 'The proles are not human beings', he said carelessly.[30]

Death, poverty and unhappiness *are* eliminable by conceptual revisions, if we choose to say so, and the more easily because all three notions have a moral force that doublethinkers seek to think away. The fact that they can't be thought away (and Orwell's own story turns on the impossibility of redescribing the unendurable) is our last, painful exit from the solipsistic dream. Chesterton again:

> A man must be in some place from which he would certainly escape if he could, if he is really to realize that all things do not come from within.... Thank God for hard stones; thank God for hard facts; thank God for thorns and rocks and deserts and long years. At least I know now that I am not the best or strongest thing in the world. At least I know now that I have not dreamed of everything.[31]

The breaking-inward of an unknown Truth is something that exercised the imagination of the sensitive in the early years of the twentieth century, whether in the guise of Buchan's Space, or Bierce's Pan, or Yeats's bag of Druidic dreams,[32] or Olaf Stapledon's indifferent Titans. In each case the breaking-in reveals that human loyalties lie with the human world: what Is may turn out to be dreadful, owed no devotion by the humane heart and starkly incompatible with all we love. It is, I suspect, this fear which gives some theologians cause to turn aside from Truth, and to prefer, as it were, 'gods wrought of common stuff':

> I cannot worship what I hate
> Or serve a god I dare not know.[33]

What is significant about Orwell's story is that it reminds us that the 'human world' to which we may retreat from a loathed reality need have none of the qualities that the liberal mind prefers. Naipaul's survey of Muslim opinion in Iran, Pakistan and Indonesia convinced him that 'Islam sanctified rage':[34] the judgement is unjust as a comment on Islam through the ages, but seems fair enough in reference to the kind of 'fundamentalism' that is a deliberate denial of supposedly 'modern' or 'Western' values. Anti-realist theologians suggest that this 'fundamentalism' shows what is wrong with realism: on the contrary, it betrays exactly the same egoism as anti-realism itself. Theologians for whom 'God' names only our highest ideals personified, should remember what those ideals may be:

> Nobody has ever seen Big Brother. He is a face on the hoardings, a voice on the telescreen. We may be reasonably sure that he will never die, and there is already considerable uncertainty as to when he was born. Big Brother is the guise in which the Party chooses to exhibit itself to the world. His function is to act as a focusing point for love, fear, and reverence, emotions which are more easily felt towards an individual than towards an organization.[35]

To all this nightmare theism has its own reply, but it is one that cannot be grasped unless we risk the possibility of error. We may struggle to live decently in a world devoid of decency, but the longer we turn away from Truth for fear that it is terrible, the greater the chance that 'decency' will decay. Those who have lied once will lie again. A merely 'virtual' reality is what the powerful choose to say it is: in welcoming the return of 'magic' we forget the perils of *black* magic. There is no answer to that nightmare but to wake up into the presence of something evidently real and *other*, something more than mind and loftier than language.

THREE

TRUTH TRANSCENDING THOUGHT

***

Theology and Mental Microbes

IF THEOLOGIANS HAVE distrusted philosophy, others have distrusted theology. A 'theological' dispute, in some quarters, is one that cannot be resolved, has no practical importance, and yet absorbs the energies of people who would be better employed elsewhere. Plato's Callicles once held a similar opinion of 'philosophy'.[1] It is my contention that 'theological' – and 'metaphysical' – discourse is not all irresoluble, and has profound significance for our common lives. Even that paradigmatically 'theological' question, how many angels can dance on the point of a pin, is far from foolish. The answer is: 'as many as they please'. Angels, which are, by hypothesis, immaterial intellects, do not occupy space to the exclusion of any other such intellectual substance, and their being 'on' the point of a pin can only mean that they attend to it. The question is not one that directly concerned our medieval predecessors, although it seems as difficult to persuade anyone of this as it is to clear Canute of the charge of insane conceit. It took shape, as a parody, during the revolt against scholastic thought. The precise image of the dancing angels is found as a jest in Isaac D'Israeli's *Curiosities of Literature* (1791):

> The reader desirous of being merry with Aquinas's angels may find them in Martinus Scriblerus, in Ch. VII who inquires if angels pass from one extreme to another without going through the middle? And if angels know things more clearly in the morning? How many angels can dance on the point of a very fine needle, without jostling one another?[2]

The question, please note, does *not* appear in Martinus Scriblerus (a satirical work composed by Pope, Arbuthnot and Swift sometime before 1714), and neither does it appear in any extant medieval discussion. Aquinas does ask[3] whether a multiplicity of angels can co-exist in the same place, and there is an anonymous fourteenth-century treatise which speaks of a thousand souls in heaven sitting on the point of a needle. Someone did connect the ideas at some point in the later middle ages. Joseph Glanvill commented, in *The Vanity of Dogmatizing* in 1661: 'he that said a *thousand* [angels] might dance on the point of a Needle, spake but grossly; and we may as well suppose them to have *wings*, as a proper *Ubi*'.[4] This was an episode in a debate about whether everything that existed actually existed somewhere and was thereby 'material'. Nothing material can be in more than one place at a time without also occupying the intervening places; nor occupy successive positions discontinuously; nor permit any other thing to occupy the same space at the same time. Although the question about angels is itself a deliberate mockery, the underlying issue is one of considerable moment. 'There' (as Plotinus named Reality) there is no distance (as I shall suggest below).

Those who mock theological or philosophical discourse are themselves the victims of a theological or philosophical infection. The specific form of that infection is 'positivist': the conviction that there is nothing real except what can be measured by the instruments available to 'science', and nothing true which makes no measurable difference to our everyday perception. The positivist slogan is not itself a scientific one. In its plainest form (that all meaningful utterances are either tautologies or open to empirical test) it is, notoriously, self-refuting, since that judgement itself is neither a tautology nor open to any empirical test. It has the force of an instruction – but one that, by its makers' own account, they can supply no reason for, nor for their own authority. The one clear proof that A. J. Ayer (1910–89), sometime positivist prophet, once offered for the thought that philosophy progresses was that no one, least of all himself, now believed a word of *Language, Truth and Logic* – or rather, no professional philosopher. The trouble with mental microbes, spiritual infections, is that they continue to infect new genera-tions, long after their first victims have recovered. Unless we take serious steps to investigate the principles that move us, we shall continue in the influence of principles we could not believe true. That thought itself, which is now frequently employed against 'religion', actually has a far wider relevance. Nothing says that only the 'religious', or only 'theists', are hosts to such mental microbes. Such infections are exactly why philosophers have urged us to 'spring clean' our minds: not that nothing should ever be believed unless it can be demonstrated to everyone's satisfaction, but that we should occasionally put our ordinary beliefs on hold, even if we must, in the end, accept them without proof. An occasional spring clean at least gives us some chance of clearing out infections – and discovering things we thought we'd lost forever.

'Mental microbes' are what many have called the stray opinions which infest our minds.[5] More recently, Dawkins' expression 'memes' has won support, together with assorted memes (or microbes) about the way 'religions' spread themselves. 'Meme-eaters' have also been identified: spreading infections which demolish earlier memes, and leave us 'clear'. Earlier ages talked instead of driving out the demons – and taking care lest other, and worse, demons take up residence instead. There may be scope for thinking of the mystical 'pure consciousness', to which (perhaps) both Buddhists and Pyrrhonian sceptics have sometimes aspired. Maybe we can occasionally become aware of something more than memes, or microbes. Maybe we sometimes silence them. Such exercises are not foolish ones, and may often use familiar philosophical antinomies to show our limits. But there are other routes to sense: not silence, but true speech. 'Science', being the construction of critical experiments to test hypotheses against results, is not much different in form from other scholarly or critical enquiry. What we need to do is see what implications theories have, and try them out. We may always have good reason to remember that our past successes do not guarantee the future: all we can often say is that we've managed to cope so far. My exposition of the arguments for theism is almost always of that critical kind: simply to show that the alternatives collapse. It does not follow that any particular sort of theism is certainly true: maybe there are more alternatives than I have yet perceived; maybe the choice between some different versions is, for now, impossible. But if the arguments are good ones, it will be worth seeing for how long we can live as theists, prayerfully. Perhaps the experiment will fail, but not because it is too hospitable to memes: on the contrary, theism itself is a meme-eater, and as hostile as any to the accumulation of opinions. If (and I would argue only if) theism is true, we have a right to trust our philosophical capacities – when honestly engaged – to lead us through.

The Perils of Philosophy

Unfortunately, our philosophical investigations may instead engender an unhealthy arrogance, a conviction that 'we know the answers, and are not deceived'. In saying this, I am within a long intellectual tradition, and one that has itself had some effect on common opinions about philosophy. 'Philosophy teaches us to speak with an appearance of truth on all things, and causes us to be admired by the less learned.[6] Descartes was not the first (nor yet the last) to complain that academic philosophizing was betraying a trust. It is a familiar philosophical trope – one that positivists and their present-day opponents both indulge – to denigrate the earlier infections just because they're earlier. 'Postmoderns', declaring that they have abandoned 'modernist' delusions (as that the later must be better than the earlier), make clear their own modernity by saying that they're later (and so better) than 'the modern'. All intellectuals, including scientists, progress by correcting or dismissing earlier intellectuals. Many an 'introduction to philosophy', as I pointed out before, is simply a prolonged account of all the fallacies and false beliefs (alleged) of earlier writers, without any hint that those writers might have caught a glimpse of something true. It is not necessarily an entirely bad idea – or may at least be better than the usual alternative (which is to assume that all those in authority speak with authority). The problem is to avoid Chesterton's wry comment: 'with all politeness I propose not to be bullied with long words instead of short reasons, or consider your business a triumphant progress merely because you're always finding out that you were wrong'.[7] True philosophy is the attempt to discover, perhaps to recover, wisdom. That is why, so Philo of Alexandria tells us, the High Priest must strip off the soul's tunic of opinion and imagery to enter the Holy of Holies[8] – not so as to show ourselves more knowing, as less trusting, than our neighbours. This was Descartes' project, and his hope, explicitly, was that he might thereby secure as knowledge what piety already had endorsed. 'For although it is quite enough for us faithful ones to accept by means of faith the fact that the human soul does not perish with the body, and that God exists, it certainly does not seem possible ever to persuade infidels of any religion, indeed, we may almost say, of any moral virtue, unless, to begin with, we prove these two facts by means of natural reason'.[9]

If discovering or recovering wisdom is the point of philosophical enquiry, it is still true that the method is Philo's, and that it is not easy to strip ourselves of fashionable opinions. The chances are high that those who think themselves most free of 'prejudice' are most deeply infected with whatever microbes are endemic. Offering them the tools of dialectic may only encourage the feeble cynicism that sometimes passes for maturity: still worse, it may lead to despair. Perhaps we should remember Epictetus' warning, that one who pretends to 'teach philosophy' without the knowledge, virtue and the strength of soul to cope with distressed and corrupted souls, 'and above all the counsel of God advising him to occupy this office'[10] is a vulgarizer of the mysteries, a quack doctor:

> The affair is momentous, it is full of mystery, not a chance gift, nor given to all comers.... You are opening up a doctor's office although you possess no equipment other than drugs, but when or how these drugs are applied you neither know nor have ever taken the trouble to learn.... Why do you play at hazard in matters of the utmost moment? If you find the principles of philosophy entertaining sit down and turn them over in your mind all by yourself, but don't ever call yourself a philosopher.[11]

The lessons that philosophers ought to rehearse (so Epictetus said), to write down daily and to put into practice, are the primacy of individual moral choice, the relative unimportance of body, rank and estate, and the knowledge of what is truly their own and what is permitted them.[12] That was the wisdom that philosophers sought to recover for themselves, while doubting that any of us could handle it for long.

That sort of philosopher is defined as one who glimpses 'as through a narrow crack' the divine reality.[13] Till we have done so, and so shaken free of the false glamour and fake terrors of this world, we shall not even be freemen: we are slaves until we are ready to die by torture if it is our job. [14] It seems an alarming prospect: quite apart from the pain envisaged, it is all too easy to believe that we are indispensable, that nothing can go right without our guidance (so we must surely live). At least (less mockingly) it's easier to die for a cause that is not ruined by one's dying for it – but how shall we believe it's not? Epictetus himself confessed that he and his disciples were, as it were, Jews in word but not in deed: 'not dyed-in-the-wool Jews', very far from applying the principles they teach: 'so although we are unable even to fulfil the profession of man, we take on the additional profession of the philosopher'. [15]

Most of us had probably better be content as sophists or as state-kept schoolmen, licensed to lay out the tools, but not to use them. Epictetus' challenge remains: 'even if you are not yet Socrates, you ought to live as one who wishes to be Socrates'. [16] Central to that challenge is the significance of Truth, and its difference from the dream.

The Significance of Truth

There are those who have despaired of Truth (and maybe with good reason). Even some theologians have come to believe (as I have already outlined) that the best way of understanding and developing the theological tradition is to join hands with those who doubt that there is any Truth, apart from what 'we' say and do. The choice for them is only, what story shall we tell ourselves and others? My contention is that this is exactly the wrong move.

The First Noble Truth of theism (and of common sense) is the reality of Truth itself. Some who think, as I do, that Truth, or Being, or Reality, is the first thing to be known, have been inclined to blame Descartes, or Augustine, or Socrates himself, for concentrating on the reality of self, rather than on that reality in which, or over against which, we are thinking things. That, it is said, is the route to solipsism, the inability to see the real being of any 'other' thing than the bare self. There is maybe a truth in this rebuke: it is certainly easy to think so when confronted by such solipsists (for whom 'subjectivity is the only divinity'). [17] But it may also be that our awareness of the Truth is rightly mediated through awareness of our selves. 'We are to stop our ears and convert our vision and our other senses inwards upon the Self.'[18] Or, in Augustine's words:

> Let the mind know itself and not seek itself as if it were absent; let it fix the attention of its will, by which it formerly wandered over many things, upon itself, and think of itself. So it will see that there never was a time when it did not love itself, and never a time when it did not know itself.[19]

That waking self is not self-evidently identical with Descartes or Augustine: its being lay in thinking (or as a later, Irish, Cartesian said, in perceiving, willing, acting).[20] It must always know itself: 'where could my heart flee from my heart? Where could I flee from my own self?'[21] If you deny that you have a will, as Augustine observed, you have dropped out of the conversation: 'because I do not have to answer your questions unless you want to know what you are asking. Furthermore if you have no desire to attain wisdom, there should be no discussion with you about such matters. Finally, you can be no friend of mine if you do not wish me well.'[22]

The very act of doubting revealed the Self as sometimes, or as possibly, mistaken. What Descartes realized (and others, no doubt, before him) was that this revealed a truth: namely, that there was indeed a Truth by which his thought was measured. Maybe nothing that I ordinarily suppose is true: so be it, but in that case there is still a Truth, unknown to me, by comparison with which my thought is false. My thought is imperfect, shifting, possibly self-contradictory, finite: but it is all these things because there is a perfect, unchangeable, coherent, infinite reality, *and I already know that it is so*. There could be no doubt, no error, unless there were a Real, nor could we entertain such doubt or recognize the notion of such error unless we already knew it. As Plato pointed out long before, I must already know what the True is if I am even to notice that my thought might not be true.[23] 'The woman who had lost a coin searched for it by the light of a lantern, but she would never have found it unless she had remembered it',[24] nor known that she had lost it.

The first noble truth of metaphysical theism is just this. 'Truth exists: the sole purpose of this proposition is to assert the

existence of truth against imbeciles and sceptics.'[25] The idea that
there is no reality cannot even be coherently expressed, nor yet
the idea that what is true depends only upon what 'we' say.
Truth, or Being, or Reality is what theologians have first in mind
in speaking of God. According to the first American philosopher
of note (and hell-fire preacher), Jonathan Edwards (1703–58),
the central act of faith is 'the cordial consent of beings to Being in
general', which is to say, to God.[26] He spoke within an ancient,
and unduly neglected, tradition, from which we may take three
examples. The poet Gerard Manley Hopkins (1844–89) on
Parmenides: 'His great text, which he repeats with religious
conviction, is that Being is and Not-being is not – which perhaps
one can say, a little over-defining his meaning, means that all
things are upheld by instress and are meaningless without it.'[27]
Augustine: 'I had promised to show you, if you recall, that there
is something higher than our mind and reason. There you have it
– truth itself! Embrace it if you can and enjoy it.'[28] Or as the
French philosopher Nicolas Malebranche (1638–1715) put it:
'the truth is uncreated, immutable, immense, eternal and above
all things. It is true by itself. It draws its perfection from no other
thing. It renders creatures more perfect and all minds naturally
seek to know it. Only God can have all these perfections.
Therefore, truth is God.'[29]

The philosophers in question claim that Truth, and its
unchangeability, immensity, infinity and all the rest, are necessary postulates of reason. Those who choose to say instead that
'Truth' is only what we choose to think, and that realists are
therefore *wrong*, have left the path of reason. Maybe that
departure is permissible – though if it is, traditional attacks on
'faith' seem quite beside the point. If it's all right to abandon
reason in the interests of a 'truth' which we create, then there is
no obstacle to making a *religious* truth, for good or ill. Our
evidence is that this is likelier to be popular, and more long-
lasting, than secular ideology.

The Meaning of Truth

It is evidently true that philosophical theists have spoken of
Truth, Being or Reality as God. There can be nothing real

outside Reality, nor can anything be worth more than the Truth. At this stage in the argument, nothing more surprising is being said of it than, simply, that reality is real. Whatever else is true, there is an Is (as Chesterton put it). I shall add further theorems in the following chapters. What is it that is being claimed, and what is it like to deny it?

First, I must distinguish Truth from what is true: 'being true' is an attribute of statements, or else of propositions. The same statement (for example: I am sitting down) is sometimes true, and sometimes not (true when said by someone who is sitting down, and not otherwise). When it *is* true, this is by virtue of things being as it's said they are. A is truly said of b just if b (at that time and place) is A. Propositions are less changeable: whereas the same statement may be sometimes true, and sometimes not, this is precisely to say that the same statement expresses different propositions, which are unchangeably true or not-true (as that such-and-such a person is sitting down at such-and-such a time and place). In neither case, by the way, is 'not being true' the same as 'being false'. A proposition identifies the condition under which a statement counts as true (as it might be, b's being A at that particular time and place). It is, so far, an open question whether there are genuinely 'true statements': there could only be such statements if someone or other made them, and it is conceivable – though improbable – that none of the statements ever made have yet been true. It may even be an open question whether there are true propositions: do propositions have any being independent of their being considered? But even if we suppose that no one has uttered a true statement, and that there are no propositions apart from those we posit as the truth-conditions of particular token-statements, we must still admit to the reality of Truth. In fact, the very supposition, that none of our statements have been true-in-fact, and that propositions aren't independent reals, requires us to admit the notion of What Is, apart from anything we say of it. Even if we attempt to live without the commonsensical 'correspondence' account of 'being true' (that statements are true which 'correspond' to how things are), and suggest instead that statements are 'true' which fit with other 'true' statements in ways that we approve, we do no more than offer a new description of What Is. It is a condition of our meaning anything at all in what we say that we admit the possibility of being *wrong*. Knowing that we can be wrong, we know that there is something against which our words are measured – or against which we aim to measure them.

By 'Truth' I don't intend the property we hope our statements, or the propositions they express, may sometimes have, but rather the extra-linguistic reality, the abyss of being, which we cannot abandon without ceasing to make sense. That there are real difficulties in conceiving such an extra-linguistic Real, I will admit: how can we hope to describe It as It is, when any description must be couched in some particular language, and so carve up, in thought alone, the Uncarved Block? We can, commonsensically, find confirmation that things are as we say they are – but only by saying again (with what seems to us good reason) that that is how they are. Nothing could count as evidence that we were wrong in some claim or another, except another, better-attested, claim that things were different. All our descriptions, all our maps and graphs and labels, depend on us for what they are, and what counts as support for them. The Truth itself does not. We can conceive, as before, that nothing we have ever said is true – although we have no experience of what counts as 'true' except the statements that are pointed out, and firmly believed, as true. Just so, none of the things we commonly call 'people', may really be what is meant by 'people': they are indeed (let us suppose) exactly what are commonly called 'people' and yet do not have the properties connoted by that term. All efforts to evade that challenge by asserting that 'people' can only have the extension that, we may admit, it does, are open to the obvious retort that, on the same account, we cannot ever have doubted there were witches (since certainly there were creatures we *called* witches, and 'being a witch' is only 'being called one').

True statements say things as they *are*, and we believe them true insofar as we believe that things *are* as they say. It is that Being which I mean by Truth. In positing or accepting that Being (to which our statements, even if derivatively true, only gesture) we must also acknowledge It as One. Suppose there were two or more such Truths: then *that* is the Truth that there would be (in effect that there were many distinct worlds, without any physical relationship, united only in their shared participation in the single Being). The Truth is of its nature single: to think that there are two Truths, without any asymmetrical relation of derivation or dependency, is to think what can't be thought. But even saying that the Truth is One may be misleading: it is not that there might be many Truths, or that the Truth we are addressing is but one of many. By calling it One, we only mean that It is not multiple, nor one of many.

Which is, of course, what theologians have also said of God.[30] It may be possible to reject theism: the cost is higher than we sometimes think, for with it we abandon this charged notion of the single Truth, that does not depend on our descriptions of It, and which demands our loyalty. Whether we think of Truth as all the things there are, or as everything that is the case,[31] we cannot rationally deny it. Irreligion, in its first and simplest sense, is to prefer the lie.

The Duty to Discover Truth

Post-modernists believe that the appeal to Truth is superstition, or political manipulation. Apparently there are no objectively good reasons, nor any 'facts of the matter' in any judicial case, and all attempts to reach a verdict (in courts, laboratories, parliaments – or academic meetings) are only power-plays. It seems obvious that those already in authority (with access to more power) will be delighted to support that claim, since their opponents will have thrown away the one best tool of revolution: the appeal to something of more weight than they. It is one thing to draw attention to the misuse of reason, evidence and claims to truth: quite another to deny (self-defeatingly) that anything is true, or holy, or of good report. In admitting the real being of Truth, we mark our readiness to give up our dreams – and also to oppose the dreams of others. 'Post-modernity' is the expected death of reason – expected, that is, since God's death was announced (a little prematurely).

On the other hand, there are also those who think that Truth is so obvious that no appeal is necessary. Isn't its very obviousness what makes it real? What relevance can truisms have to religion? But the father of atomic science, Democritos, had a point: 'really we know nothing, for Truth is in the depths.'[32] The world of our everyday experience, structured as it is by goals and projects of an illusory kind, does not provide us with a sure foundation. We are like children building sand-castles to be washed away,[33] or dreamers. 'For those who've woken up there is one common world; each sleeper's turned aside to a private one'[34] – no less private and delusory because imagined to be shared with others of our greedy, proud and frightened sort. 'The Stoics say that every inferior man is insane, since he has ignorance of himself and of his concerns, and this is insanity.'[35] The world of fame and fortune, of everyday concerns, is, so Marcus Aurelius had warned, 'a dream and a delirium',[36] not to be taken seriously except as an occasion for discovering one's own being and the truth. 'Woe to those who turn away from (God's) light and are delighted to cling to their own darkness!'[37] The point is to wake up.

The unexamined world we casually inhabit, of lords, priests and commoners, pets and pests and prey and creepy-crawly things, the world of fame and fortune, triumph and adversity, is Aurelius's 'dream and delirium'. But why should we care to wake? Granted that Truth, Being, Reality, Substance (or whatever other label is required) is an undeniable, inescapable fact (grant that Truth is Truth), and that we commonly prefer to live 'a dream and delirium' rather than embrace that Truth, why should we change? Why should we seek to disinfect our minds, or rouse ourselves from comfortable dreams, especially if the Truth itself is alien to us? Chesterton makes a traditional reply, evoking our occasional sense of gratitude, or presence:

> There is at the back of all our lives an abyss of light, more blinding and unfathomable than any abyss of darkness; and it is the abyss of actuality, of existence, of the fact that things truly are, and that we ourselves are incredibly and sometimes almost incredulously real. It is the fundamental fact of being, as against not being; it is unthinkable, yet we cannot unthink it, though we may sometimes be unthinking about it; unthinking and especially unthanking. For he who has realized this reality knows that it does outweigh, literally to infinity, all lesser regrets or arguments for negation, and that under all our grumblings there is a subconscious substance of gratitude.[38]

'I would maintain', Chesterton had said years earlier, 'that thanks are the highest form of thought.'[39] Because thankfulness, despite everything, is appropriate, we can justly speak of that abyss of being as God. I do not deny the difficulties:

> There is one sin: to call a green leaf grey,
> Whereat the sun in heaven shuddereth.
> There is one blasphemy: for death to pray,
> For God alone knoweth the praise of death.[40]

But Chesterton himself was well aware of the temptation, and that some of us are tried past human powers to resist. Facing the facts often requires enormous courage: call it faith.

Why should we cultivate that faith, which is quite different from the sort of faith that rests in comfortable dreams? There are plenty of truths that we would rather not know; plenty that we have no reason to want to know. Why should we not prefer to live in ignorance, or bind ourselves within the realm of humanly-constructed 'truth', the world of pets and pests and prey and creepy-crawly things?

> Wherefore my brittle gods I make
> of friendly clay and kindly stone, –
> Wrought with my hands, to serve or break,
> from crown to toe, my work, my own.
> My eyes can see, my nose can smell,
> my fingers touch their painted face,
> they weave their little homely spell
> to warm me from the cold of Space.[41]

Knowing the Truth, and even knowing that there is a truth, is not guaranteed to make our lives agreeable (a point to which I shall return in a later chapter). Even if it did, this would not help to explain the traditional equation of Being and God: on the contrary, to be God is to be worshipful, and those who pretend to worship God for the sake of worldly advantages must really have another goal in mind than Him.

Either the Truth demands our worship, or it doesn't. If it does, the first dogma of the philosophical theist has been granted. If it doesn't, we may decently prefer to dream. If (as seems quite probable) a life constructed round religion is likely to bring emotional or social advantages, what is the point of deconstructing it? One might as well seek to persuade a friend that her love-life would be improved once she has ceased to think or feel that what she loves is lovely. No rational, unaffected person may suppose that Beatrice is 'beautiful', or that she differs in any significant respect from any other: falling in love with anyone at all would be as easy, and as foolish. It may also be true that many of those who 'fell in love' have ended badly (perhaps by falling out of love again), and many or most or all of those who are loved have been 'unworthy' of such wonder. But if no one at all is 'worthy', and 'loveliness' is always and only an illusion, why seek to destroy it? What is so marvellous (or lovely) about Truth, if nothing at all is lovely? 'If the belief that Bacon wrote Shakespeare gives a peace which the world cannot give, why pedantically reject such solace?'[42] What duty do we have to believe what's true, or urge others to believe, if there are no duties? We must conclude that the point of disabusing people must be that Truth is uniquely worth believing, and preferring:

> Do not all charms fly
> At the mere touch of cold philosophy?[43]

But not the charms of cold philosophy itself. But in that case, atheists must be believers: they believe, exactly, that the Truth is worth more than illusion, however comforting illusions are, and however much delight they add to what we'd otherwise feel. Even if they answer that the dangers of illusion are, occasionally, obvious, this does not explain why *all* illusions, even pleasant ones, should be dispelled. It simply is not true that every false belief (or every belief judged false by atheists) has obviously bad effects. Many such fond beliefs are what makes life worth living – at least for the irreligious. Militant atheism trades on exactly the same conviction as any proselytizing creed: that those who don't align themselves with Truth are lost, and must – for their own sake – be disabused of all their false conceptions, even if it kills them:

> 'Fool! Fool!' repeated he, while his eyes still
> Relented not, nor mov'd; 'from every ill
> Of life have I preserved thee to this day,
> And shall I see thee made a serpent's prey?'[44]

Some post-moderns, and even some modern moralists, can only answer that some of us *choose* to be aligned with 'Truth', at whatever personal cost, or else that we call 'Truth' what we have chosen. In choosing to describe the world only in 'objective' terms, without acknowledging any symbolic meaning, or animistic sympathy, we have, in effect, constructed a 'real world' that has no human properties at all, and so is not 'worth admiring'. Whereas older moralists supposed that natural kinds should be kept separate, or that moral pollution brought real risks, the modern or post-modern moralist contends that nothing is 'objectively important', and that 'moral depravity' has no effect in nature. Our moral decisions, on those terms, are only our shared strategies for coping, for getting what we want (whatever that may be) at least expense. There are no morally inappropriate strategies, but only effective or ineffective ones. In which case, as Jacques Monod realized,[45] the fundamental choice to value 'the objective world', and to describe Reality without emotional affect, is only one arbitrary choice, without 'real value' (since 'real value' is as much as to say 'round square', or 'gaseous vertebrate').

Objectivism and the Love of Truth

C. S. Lewis's concern, in *That Hideous Strength* and also in *The Abolition of Man*, was to explore the practical implications of the objectivism that infected (and infects) the intellectual landscape of the twentieth century. That objectivism purports to be concerned with *facts*, with what can be affirmed without any moral implication or emotional import. Nothing is to count as true beyond what can be 'proved' true to the satisfaction of someone utterly indifferent to humane values. The strategy is absurd: one unconvinced by talk of intellectual duties to prefer the simplest theory capable of 'explaining' the experimental data, or to accept – even if provisionally – what researchers say those data are, will not be convinced of any factual claim. In that sense no proofs are possible that transcend the limits of the enquirer's ethics and emotions. Nor is there any 'factual' proof available for the very claim that only 'factually proven' theses are to be accepted. It must by now be obvious that 'objective truths', or truth without moral import, are only a small part of truth, and that our ethical judgements fix all the truths we find agreeable to think. Objectivism turns out to be the ideological control of language, lest we notice truths the controllers do not like. 'Objectivity', so understood, does not differ from 'total allegiance.'[46] Ingsoc is just the same as Obliteration of the Self.[47]

The larger issue of the grounds of ethics I shall address in a later chapter. Here it is only worth insisting that those of us, including atheists, who value Being will also value beings, the real things that are always more than words can say. How can we love – or even recognize – Being Itself, when we do not love, or recognize, the beings alongside us? The discovery that there are other beings in the world than ourselves is one that everyone will say that they have made, and almost no one genuinely believes. Which of us really believes that other creatures' pains or feelings are as real as ours? Really? Do we act on that belief? Or as Iris Murdoch's parodic Plato says:

> Truth isn't just facts, it's a *mode of being*. It's finding out what's real and responding to it – like when we really see other people and know they exist. You see I think there are different levels in the soul, only a bit of us is real and knows truth, the rest is fantasy, anxiety, resentment, envy, all selfish tricks – *you* know. We live in a dream, we're wrapped up in a dark veil, we think we're omnipotent magicians, we don't believe anything *exists* except ourselves.[48]

Reality, which it is reasonable to call God, contains or sustains all lesser things. Everything that is at all, is by participation in Being. Falling in love may not, after all, be falling wholly into an illusion: on the contrary, that may be the moment when we are made to realize the real being at least of one thing. However fanciful a lover's compliments may be when they are reckoned to be literal descriptions of the beloved's virtues, they may express a truth: not that the beloved is anything in particular, but simply that she IS – and the lover, for once, has noticed it. The lover, in brief, has noticed God, in one small aspect of God's Being.

Implicit in my earlier remarks is the claim that we can become aware of Truth (though not always of what is true) in those moments when we are aware of ourselves. Descartes, though he expounds the argument in successive stages, does not *first* conclude that he exists, and only then that there is an Infinite

Reality of which he is aware: the realization of his own existence is also the moment when he realizes the Infinite Real of which he is a segment, or a subject. When we are present to ourselves, it is by virtue of the Presence to us of Being. What comes to us as part of the demanding Presence is what we chiefly take as true. Was Descartes simply flattering Elizabeth of Bohemia (granddaughter of James I, exile in the Hague) in his introduction to *Principles of Philosophy*?

> I note that nothing is required for perfect and sublime wisdom either with regard to comprehension or to will which does not shine forth in your conduct. For there appears in it along with majesty a certain exceptional benevolence and gentleness which is assaulted by the perpetual injustices of fortune but never provoked or daunted. And this has conquered me to such an extent that I not only think that this Philosophy of mine ought to be dedicated and consecrated to the Wisdom which I perceive in you (because my Philosophy itself is nothing other than the study of wisdom); but that I also have no greater wish to hear myself called a Philosopher than to be called the most devoted admirer of your Most Serene Highness.[49]

In one letter he writes of being dumbstruck on speaking to her, 'seeing superhuman sentiments flowing from a body such as painters give to angels I would have been ravished like a man coming fresh from earth to heaven....'[50] Such devotion does not fit our figure of Descartes, and may be feigned: the point is that some lovers have felt that – and been content to say that the beloved is the place where Being comes alive, where they are most aware of Truth as something above rubies, and of themselves as most unworthy. No doubt a reasonable lover also knows, quite quickly, that this admiration, offered to a finite, fellow creature, is a joke. 'Viewed as enfolded absolutely in God, each thing *is* God; for *there* it is not its finite self. Viewed as unfolded from God, no thing is God; for *here* it *is* its finite, contracted self and is said to participate in God rather than to be God.'[51] That tension lies at the root of much religion, and will concern me later.

Love, or what that love too easily becomes, is not enough. Orwell's Winston, failing to find any intellectual answer to

O'Brien's anti-realism, hopes instead that merely natural passion or ancestral memory will one day overturn the Party:

> Always in your stomach and your skin there was a sort of protest, a feeling that you had been cheated of something that you had a right to.... Why should one feel it to be intolerable unless one had a kind of ancestral memory that things had once been different?[52]

Things cannot be only and entirely what the Party says as long as 'the animal instinct, the simple undifferentiated desire' exists to negate all Party hierarchies and rules. Less crudely, but to similar effect, a post-Wittgensteinian movement puts its trust in what we 'naturally' feel and say. Even if there is no 'real world' outside all human speech, there may still be limits on what human beings naturally say. Death, poverty and unhappiness are not external realities: till creatures capable of complaint emerged from nowhere there were no such evils. But now that we are here it is inevitable that we put that construction upon things, and any attempt to 'go against nature' fails. It is not clear that this response can work. If there is an ineluctable human nature, then there is a world impervious to human redescription – but that is what is in question. 'Men', says O'Brien, 'are infinitely malleable.'[53] Winston's error, as Orwell depicts it, is twofold. On the one hand, the Party's hierarchy itself rests on natural emotions with as good a claim to permanence as undifferentiated lust (namely, the will to power).[54] On the other, lust itself can be destroyed as surely as family feeling: 'There were things, your own acts, from which you could not recover. Something was killed in your breast: burnt out, cauterized.'[55]

An alternative is offered Winston: the music of a thrush 'as though it were a kind of liquid stuff that poured all over him and got mixed up with the sunlight that filtered through the leaves.'[56] ' "He wasn't singing to us," said Julia. "He was singing to please himself. Not even that. He was just singing." '[57] Instead of the 'boot stamping on the human face – forever' that O'Brien imagines,[58] Winston hopes for 'a race of conscious beings' that must one day come from the loins of the 'solid unconquerable figure, made monstrous by work and child-bearing, toiling from birth to death and still singing'.[59] Lust and purposeless song alike are offered as answers to the rationalist impasse (though

Winston also seeks to ally himself with the imagined future by keeping the mind alive, and 'pass[ing] on the secret doctrine that two plus two makes four').[60] 'By foreknowledge...one could mystically share in [the imagined future, where there is no darkness].'[61] If thought is limited by language, and the Party controls language and public record, then the only breach in the walls must be wordless, and so thoughtless. If all meanings are subject to change, then it is the sheer alien facticity of things that must remain.

Considered as merely 'natural' such song is just as malleable, as redescribable, as any other response. What Orwell may have intended, nonetheless, was something more than 'natural': 'the bird-song from the timeless world reminds the listener that the soul's situation in the time-state is that of exile....Birds and their voices have been held oracular from the beginning of time.'[62] Coincidentally, it is the otherness and indifference of a passing bird that, Murdoch says, can lift our spirits out of self-absorption.[63] It is not inappropriate that angels, messengers of God, have been imagined winged.[64] In Chesterton's words:

> How much larger your life would be if yourself could become smaller in it; if you could really look at other men with common curiosity and pleasure; if you could see them walking in their sunny selfishness and their virile indifference! You would begin to be interested in them, because they were not interested in you![65]

Our exile is Aurelius's 'dream and delirium'. Our – partial – escape is by awakening to facts, and maybe by remembering (as Plato said). Love and delight, as part of the human world, are too easily corrupted or destroyed – but they may still give us a clue to the right response to Being, and some hint of Its true nature.

FOUR

NECESSITY AND UNITY

***

Necessity and Explanation

THE SECOND NOBLE truth is that the Truth, that God, 'exists necessarily'. Reality is not something that 'just happens to exist', that 'might not exist'. Neither does it 'just happen' to be what fundamentally it is. That this is so can be realized by examining the fashionable alternative. It is widely claimed, in modern philosophical circles, that nothing can exist by its own necessity, that there is nothing whose properly conceived nature requires it to exist. Something, it is said, is wrong with the very idea of such a 'necessary being' (whose essence and existence coincide), and therefore with the God of the Philosophers. On this account, whatever exists must exist because of something else than its own nature, or for no reason. To explain something's existence, that is, we must refer to some other existent thing's nature, or fail to find any explanation. So all explanations of a thing's existence either end in an infinite regress (which is no true explanation) or in no explanation at all.[1]

Not all infinite regresses are 'vicious' ones, but an 'explanation' of that sort is not an explanation. If A exists only because of B, and B only because of C (and so on forever), then the whole infinite chain of circumstance itself (*pace* David Hume) demands an explanation, or shows that there is none. So let us suppose that there is something (either some one thing or the total chain of circumstance) that exists without any explanation at all, that 'just is'. If there is such a thing that can exist without explanation, what could it be? People sometimes assume that something rather simple (a hydrogen atom or an undifferentiated singularity) might be meant: but by hypothesis it can be nothing in the thing's conceived nature that enables it to come into being without an explanation whereas other things (with different natures) could not. Whatever 'comes into being' could not come into being because its nature, uniquely, allowed it to:

until it came into being there was no such nature. Alternatively, Plato was entirely right and 'natures' exist before and independently of what 'possesses' them (whether necessarily or not) – but in that case, there may, after all, be a nature that demands instantiation (which is what has been denied). Such a nature would be permanently realised: if the nature of the real thing explains its being, there can be no time when it does not exist (or else there is some other explanation of its being than its mere nature). If, on the other hand, there are no natures that require instantiation, then anything at all can exist without explanation.[2] And if everything can exist without explanation, then nothing ever explains a thing's existence (because x is no explanation of y if y could exist anyway). If everything conceivable can exist without explanation then so might Terry Pratchett's Discworld.[3] A world where (literally) anything could happen, for no intelligible reason, is not intelligible at all. If the Truth is such as to be intelligible, there must be a reason *why* it is whatever it is. So either there is something that exists (and never needed to come into existence) because of what it is, or there is no explanation at all for anything.

Might it not be that something that does not strictly *need* to exist has nonetheless existed forever, and so never needed to begin (which it could not)? Might it not be that something has existed for all the time there ever was, even though nothing has existed for longer than a finite stretch of time? Might there have been no 'very first moment' nor any 'coming into being' of the cosmic whole, because – as we look back in time – each earlier moment contains more discriminable sub-moments (so that an infinite sequence of discriminable moments precedes any moment that we pick, even though there have been only a finite number of moments of any particular length)?[4] None of this makes any difference to the earlier argument. It may be (so far) that the cosmos itself exists because it must, because its nature is to Be, and to unfold in whatever way in fact it does. Whether the cosmos has lasted for infinitely many seconds, or has lasted for infinitely many moments (as described before), or has a finite period, we still need an explanation for its being what it is. Being itself requires no explanation: there is no possibility of Absolute Non-Being. But the question remains: what will explain the kinds of being there are, the kind of Being there Is? Simply saying that it's always been like this, is not an explanation – any more than talking of 'the law of gravity' explains why apples fall, or bodies in general 'gravitate'. The Law of Gravity is no more (and no less) an explanation than Molière's 'dormitive faculty' explains why opium is soporific. Once again, if there is something that has existed 'forever', but for no reason, we cannot reasonably expect it to go on existing. Indeed, it is baffling that it still exists, since there is no reason why it should. We might as well suppose, with Pratchett, that the world does rest upon a turtle's back, and that in turn upon another turtle: if it were really 'turtles all the way down' (as the story has it) would we think that did not demand an explanation? Would it make it better if it were only one, infinitely large, turtle?

It is also worth acknowledging that there are serious difficulties with the notion that *time* has been 'for ever', that we have already always completed an infinite array of seconds: but that debate would take too long to settle.[5] The notion of an infinite 'totality' of moments, or of momentary states, is dubious. As I shall argue later, we would also need an explanation for the similarity of all such moments.

Oddly, some of the same thinkers who take it for granted that 'existence is always contingent' seek to show that 'the cosmos' *has* to be the way it is. As long as it is conceivable that there be nothing at all, we lack a complete and satisfactory explanation of things as they are. Some cosmologists[6] have accordingly sought to show that an imagined pre-cosmic Nothing nonetheless has character enough to demand the eventual emergence of particular differences. Jonathan Edwards answered this a long time ago: 'If any man thinks he Can think well Enough how there should be nothing I'll Engage that what he means by nothing is as much something as any thing that ever He thought of in his Life.'[7] The unanswered question will still be: what is it about such a pre-cosmic Nothing that requires it to be?

The Single Infinite Being

Let's start again. There are things whose conceived natures explain why they do *not* exist (round squares, for example, or – perhaps – perpetual motion). So may it not be that (for example) godless worlds or empty worlds are similarly impossible? Something must be the case. It is not possible for Not-Being to be, though it looks as if there might *be* nothing:

> It seems strange sometimes to me that there should be Being from all Eternity; and I am ready to say, What need was there that any thing should be? I should then ask myself, Whether it seems strange that there should be either Something, or Nothing? If so, it is not strange that there should BE; for the necessity of there being Something, or Nothing, implies it.[8]

Those who say that existence must always be contingent have one argument on their side: we can tell that any one particular thing exists by noticing how different the world would be if it did not. A world without tigers is noticeably different from one with tigers, so we know what it would be for 'tigers to exist' precisely because we can envisage their not existing. So it must be possible to conceive a world without a particular thing, and work out, at least in outline, what other differences must then be imagined. I can be sure (Googols apart) that my wife does exist, because my situation would be entirely different if she did not. We can demonstrate that there are black holes by identifying the difference they make: observable features that would be unlikely or inexplicable if there were no such black holes. Whatever I can conceive to exist I can also conceive not to exist, or not to have existed ever. It seems to follow that none of the things that currently exist, and no combinations of those things, are necessary: any of them, and all of them, might not have been. Even if – as some have supposed – nothing at all in this world could be different unless the world itself were different in every detail, still it must be possible to specify what other shapes the world might take, or have taken. Accordingly, it's said, there are no necessary beings.

But this argument is plainly question-begging. We have already seen good reason why we must suppose that Being Is, and could not be supposed to Not-Be. All the subsequent argument shows is that any finite existent might or might not exist, and that the total aggregate of finite existents is also unnecessary. This does not establish that there are no necessary existents: only that there are no necessary finite ones. And once

again, the very fact that we 'demonstrate' a finite thing's existence by pointing to features that would be 'unlikely or inexplicable' without it, requires that we believe there should be
explanations. If there are explanations then there is something
that must be, or Being Itself must have a definite character.

To summarize: if there is to be a genuine explanation of
anything, the explanation must terminate in a demonstration
that such-and-such is inevitable. There must be something that
could not be otherwise. But every finite existent (which class
includes the 'infinitely large, but otherwise finite, turtle'!), just
because it is conceived as one thing amongst many, could be
conceived to be absent, or entirely different. If that is true of any
single such existent it must also be true of every aggregate – even
an infinite aggregate (if such were possible) – of such existents.
So no particular finite thing is necessary, and neither is the
presumed totality of finite things. All that could be necessary is a
single infinite reality, such that no alternative to it is strictly
conceivable. If there were no such Infinite and Necessary Being
there could be no explanations.

One response might be to insist that such a Necessary Being
could not explain at all, unless it had – as above – a definite
character that excluded certain imaginable stories. And if It has
such a character (rather than imaginable others) must that in
turn not be a brute fact, or one that requires another explanation? But this is a confusion: we may be able to *imagine* other
possibilities, including ones that – so it turns out – cannot be
conceived. Maybe, for example, there can be no 'godless' worlds,
because a 'godless world' is as incoherent as a round square: we
can speak of 'round squares', and anyone can – in a sense –
know what we mean. But insofar as they do know what we
mean, they know that there can be none. The Necessary
Character of Being (whatever it turns out to be) can be described
without supposing that there are intelligible alternatives and that
(accordingly) Its character is not necessary after all.

The Unity of Being

My demonstration that there is something which must be, if
there are to be any explanations, and that this Necessary Being

cannot be a finite thing nor any aggregate of finite things, requires one further gloss. In speaking of 'the cosmos' we assume that there really is a single entity, whose nature is universal. Might that cosmos not itself be necessary, since it cannot be an aggregate, a heap? But that notion (that there is indeed *a cosmos*) is itself contentious. If we were, ordinarily, confronted by a heap of oddments why should we assume that any of the oddments shared a single nature, or that we could learn about a distant bit by looking at the more convenient bits close-by? In seeking an explanation for the overall character of the heap we would wish to know why exactly *these* bits had been piled together, or why bits of these various types. But even if we had such a general explanation (they are, let us suppose, the aggregated wastebins of a hundred households), why should we suppose that there would be a 'representative sample' of the heap, or that such a sample could be located just by examining the nearest patch? Even the assumption of rough homogeneity goes beyond the evidence.

If the cosmos were simply 'everything that happens – for its various reasons – to be the case' what guarantees that there is any single reason for what is the case, or that things here-now are representative of things far away and long ago? What sort of evidence could we have of that? Even within the framework of scientific theory it has been proposed that there are 'other universes' with quite different characters, or that the 'laws of nature' even within a universe change over time. Even geometrical truths, conceived as being reports about the measurement of actual spaces, may be quite different elsewhere: space itself, it has been postulated, can be 'bent' – which is to say that we can't say whether or when the internal angles of an actual triangle add up to 180 degrees. We may hope, of course, that all such differences will really be no more than variations on a theme, and themselves have explanations. But unless there is, somewhere, a *single* explanation for every such actual difference, and one that excludes at least the imaginable possibility that there are no identities at all between what happens *here* and *there*, our 'cosmos' is no more than an aggregate. If we are to have a realistic hope of extrapolating any local results to cover the totality, there must be something that is the same for all times and places. Somehow the 'heap' must be a single whole.

Whatever it is that makes the heap a whole is more than physical science could accommodate. For even if there were some single description, couched in terms of atoms or quarks or strings or what-you-will, that applied (how could we tell?) to every part of the material world, that description would not tell us anything about the other 'levels' of existence. Maybe we could, in principle, deduce the different forms of chemical interaction from the sub-atomic. Maybe we could even deduce what biochemical interactions (*aka* life) were allowed, or even required. But no one can seriously suppose that it is the laws of *physics* which determine what books achieve bestseller status, or what that achievement feels like to a late twentieth-century human, or what worth those books may have. I will touch upon the issue of 'emergence' in a later chapter: here it is enough to note that there are many large-scale descriptions of what happens that are not readily, or possibly, reducible to physical-law descriptions. The question then arises: how do these descriptions, these different and apparently distinct cuts through the world, relate to the one world we must believe in? Considered as the aggregate of all the things there are, the cosmos need not be and even cannot be 'the same' throughout; considered as the aggregate of all the true descriptions that there are, what says that those descriptions have any logical connection? And if there are no such connections, how can the aggregate make sense? Believing in 'emergence' (the coming-to-be of properties with no logical, or mathematical, connection to those of the components) is believing in something that 'just happens because it does' – and so abandoning the hope of explanation.

We must assume that the cosmos – both the totality of all the things there are, and the totality of everything that is the case – is more than aggregate, even if we don't know why. Is this a reply to the earlier demonstration that an aggregate of finite, contingent things, must itself be as contingent, and that 'the cosmos itself' (as being that aggregate) cannot possess the sort of necessity required of a real Explanation? If we have to assume that the cosmos is more than an aggregate, might it not after all be just that Necessary Being we have sought? We may not yet know what Nature it is that demands that things be as they are: we may not even know how it is that they are. This universe (the one that is expanding from a singularity, with just these ratios of strong force, weak force, gravity and electromagnetism) is only one conceivable possibility, only one dice-throw. But maybe the totality of such sister-worlds is the final context for all explanations, and the Necessary Existent. On this account, each separate universe is only the embodiment of one real possibility: all that is necessary is that there be all possibilities. The notion is currently a popular one (for poor reasons as well as good), but it is hardly one to be welcomed. If all possibilities are realized (somewhere) we have no way of knowing which are realized here: if the relation of the four great forces I just mentioned could indeed be arbitrarily different, then perhaps, not far away, they are. Insisting that they have been 'fixed' in the first few moments of this universe is itself an appeal to the real unity of this world here which has been thrown into doubt by extending the cosmic horizon. It is no more sensible, *a priori*, to suppose that 'this universe' is a unity than to suppose that a randomly selected acre from a wider prairie is a real unit – or that a prairie is. Such lines are ones *we* draw, and we have no firm assurance that the world has already drawn them. If there are any singularities where familiar 'laws' must fail, we have no way of telling what laws apply to where. The Many-Worlds hypothesis amounts to just that abandonment of real explanation I addressed before: 'we need not find an explanation for any particular event or entity since everything that can be conceived to happen does'. But the point of explanation is to show why some things don't.

So if we are to get much profit from our 'explanations' we must find some way in which the cosmos can be conceived as single. What is it that guarantees a uniformity (at some appropriate level of description) throughout the actual world, to make it something more than a mere heap? We dare not suppose that 'everything which can happen, does': on the one hand, why should it? on the other, if that is so, then nothing at all requires or could get an explanation. The present sidereal universe, currently conceived as expanding from a singularity, a finite span of years ago, may well not be the only one (though anything we say about the others is as metaphysical a speculation as any that our predecessors offered about angels). What is at issue, for this or for the imagined totality of serial universes is:

what ensures their unity? We must, if there are to be useful explanations, assume that the world is unified: how can it be?

Matter and the Immaterial

The problem is more than an empirical one. In the first place, we cannot demonstrate, empirically, that the world *is* one. Every failed generalization is followed, in scientific circles, by a more refined conclusion: not all swans are white, but all swans of a certain sort are white, and all swans have a particular range of colours. Maybe even quarks behave differently in different areas of the universe, but if they do it is because the underlying sameness of their being, and of the universe's being, demands that difference. We do not discover, but assume, that there is a real unity. In the second place, it is not just an empirical discovery that places differ, and that kinds may too. After all, that is the very definition of a place: that it is different from all others. Considered as a *material* universe this is one composed of (infinitely?) many distinct times and places: each locus is different from every other. What is true at one locus need not be true elsewhere, and often isn't. Loci, of course, may be differently delimited: the inside of this room, on Sunday 17th August, can itself be divided into different spatial and temporal segments (say, the north-west quarter in the afternoon). There may be some limit to the division: maybe there is a smallest possible actual segment (the diameter of an electron; the time it takes for an electron to jump from one shell to another), or maybe (as our modes of measurement suggest, as well as successive experience of yet smaller postulated particles) there is no limit of division, and each segment contains infinities. Either way, the universe considered as 'material' is axiomatically un-unified.

The problem is worse for us than for our predecessors. The ancients, understandably, supposed that light was instantaneously present everywhere its influence reached. As soon as the sun's disc passed the horizon, east and west were simultaneously (as far as we could tell) illuminated. In light the material universe found a sort of unity. In modern terms the speed of light is finite: a solar flare would light up Jupiter a long time after it lit up the moon. For light itself the passage is still instantaneous: an observing eye that rode along with light would experience all regions that it reached together, although its experience would be of many different times as well as places. There are two implications, both of which are damaging for any claim to unity. First, all spatio-temporal locations present on the track of one particular light-trail are, from that point of view, simultaneous: a different set of such locations, simultaneous from another light-trail's point of view, may easily share a location. So if all such lines of sight could be considered together, all spatio-temporal locations would be simultaneous. The fact that they can't be identifies a serious problem: it rather seems that there are innumerably many inconsistent orderings of times and places. Second, the fact (as currently supposed) that light's speed is unsurpassable (leaving aside such imagined particles as tachyons) means that there are regions of our universe that have not been, and probably never will be, in touch with each other since the universe began expanding. There will never be time enough for light from Over There to reach to Here. As a material expanse the universe does not form a coherent, communicating whole, in which what happens Here affects what happens There, wherever Here and There may be. Much of this universe, in other words, is utterly beyond empirical discovery – unless there is after all some deeper unity, imaged in the ancient talk of 'light', but not identical with electro-magnetic radiation. The cosmos, whatever its limits, cannot be 'God's Body' (as some recent theologians have thought it easy to suggest) unless there is indeed some non-material unity.

Science fantasists (by which I mean both science fiction writers and speculative cosmologists) have sometimes wondered whether there are connections that transcend light's sluggish passage, or whether there is another 'hyperspace' where all times and places are coincident. These fantasies (which may indeed prove true) are welcomed, in part, because we need to suppose there is a unity that somehow transcends the *a priori* difference of times and places, and the *a posteriori* dislocation created by the slowness of light's passage. The trouble with such metaphors is that they don't solve the problem.

If all regions of this universe are 'united' by trans-light connections, whether through an imagined resonance of particles (the Bell–Rosen–Podalsky effect)[9] or through their being each aligned to a single point of hyperspace, we have an explanation (of a sort) for the otherwise inexplicable uniformity we are bound to postulate. If different regions are, as they must be, different, why should they ever be found to be the same? What is it that guarantees, on the other hand, that differences in one region must be accompanied by differences elsewhere? Why should we expect the 'whole' to move together? Even the passage of light, so far as it is a passage, merely compounds the problem: why should an alteration in a track of light here-now have any relationship to an alteration elsewhere down the trail? The connections between different regions cannot be envisaged as the effect of 'travelling messengers', since the unity of the messengers along their route is also called in question. The very idea that there is a single, simple thing (a photon) is in question: maybe there are only successive disturbances in different areas of space–time (as a wave progresses up the beach without itself being one continuing, moving body of water droplets). If one region can affect another then messages can travel: but this does not explain how one region does affect another, since travelling messages involve exactly such an effect. It may seem that Bell–Rosen–Podalsky links and hyperspatial identities at least avoid that circularity. If there are such links they are not constituted by a travelling message, one that must be assumed to pass through all regions in-between the ones to be linked. The trouble is that, by the same token, they are not material links. In the material universe there is nothing that can be at separate times and places without being at all the times and places in-between. Whatever occupies one defined region thereby prevents its occupation by another, separate thing. The only sorts of thing that can dance everywhere at once, 'without jostling one another', are angels.

The unity of any material whole, in brief, cannot be founded just in continuity, in the feature whereby every region of space–time is next door to another. Insofar as such regions are different, travelling messengers depend on, and do not explain, the unity. This is also the argument which our predecessors used to demonstrate the need for a non-material entity to unify the living body: if there were no such non-material unifier, present in all the different bits, then bodies were only regions of a wider realm, as arbitrarily divided from that realm as acres in a prairie. The same was thought of the cosmos: nothing material could bind it into one, since the binding power of anything material was also called in question. There is no material glue to make one thing of many, since the glue itself needs to be glued on. That is the real point of fantastic stories about the turtles on which the earth is carried: no such explanation helps, since just the same defects will be present in the turtle as in the earth itself, to prevent their being self-supporting. The unity of living beings, and universes, must rest in something immaterial.

One effort to avoid the implication amounts to a retreat from realism. Maybe things *aren't* united after all, except in our descriptions. That one punctiform particular, one space–time locus, is 'the same' as any other is only a manner of speaking: it is only that we've marked the two loci. The point is usually expressed by saying that we 'call them the same thing', and that – outside the text – is nothing nameable. 'With words the world was called out of the empty air':[10] but words themselves are no more than marks, imitating the scent-markers or the scratches that non-linguistic animals impose. There are other worlds carved out of the Uncarved Block, by other creatures, without any need of speech. There is a truth in that. But the trouble with the theory in its fully non-realist form is that it is both unrealistic (obviously) and inconsistent. That it is unrealistic ought to be enough to count against it: even those who announce the doctrine most dogmatically do not really believe that zodiacal signs (made one by 'our' description) are as real as stars, nor that there is nothing at all to choose between descriptions such as 'child' or 'family segment' or 'collection of spare parts'. The anti-realist case, in any case, is inconsistent: if two loci are 'the same' only because they carry 'the same mark', how do we analyse the sameness of the marks? Realistically, and commonsensically, we cannot avoid admitting that there are real unities: we recognize more units than we make. And therefore must admit that there are principles of unity, within the cosmos, and for the cosmos as a whole.

The Omnipresence of the Necessary Being

My argument has been that we can only explain anything if our explanation eventually comes to rest in something that is necessarily real. That Necessary Being cannot be any finite thing, whose non-existence is conceivable. Nor can it be an aggregate of finite things, severally and collectively contingent. It may be true, so far, that what is necessary just is the widest cosmos (whether this is the present sidereal universe or some imagined larger realm), but that cosmos cannot then be conceived as an aggregate, nor a material expanse. If our attempts at explanation are to be useful we must assume that there is a unifying force in everything that is. That unifying force cannot be a material one, since all material things themselves need unification. Light was conceived, by our predecessors, as a sort of image (or an instance) of the omnipresent mind that held all things together. Our own understanding of light, or its physical substrate, has led to an increased doubt about how things hold together, which has generated its own fantasies. The moral is again that nothing strictly material serves to unify matter: nothing could make materially different things one that was itself merely material, since exactly the same problem remains unsolved.

What makes the universe one (and so makes explanation possible) is the Omnipresence of Necessary Being: as far as That is concerned no times and places are different. It is all too easy for us to believe that reality is what is spread out in time and space, the field of all our earthly endeavours. That realm has its own reality, but it can itself subsist only because every point in it is just as close to the One Being as any other. The differences between times and places are only different aspects of the One, different selections from Its fecundity. If it were not so, there would be no intelligible cosmos. The Truth we must acknowledge (and revere), by reference to which all lesser propositions and thought forms have what truth they have, is something non-material and necessary.

This may seem a dry conclusion: if that is all that theism means, some say, then what's the use of talking misleadingly about God? The totality of truth can have no other explanation for its being than what is true, than itself. Is it true that we desire to know it? Is it best addressed as being itself a sort of subject,

person, spirit? Or must it, in its total being, be entirely unlike all
lesser beings? 'Persons', it is said, are only a particular sort of
animal, existing as they do because of evolutionary aeons and at
the expense of swarming ecosystems. Truth itself, or the source
of Truth, can't be a thing like that (any more than the Stuff of
things can be ordinary water): there can be no 'persons' until
those evolutionary aeons have gone past, until there is a complex
system busily at work on earth and in the heavens. 'God' does
not, cannot name a person. And of course, for orthodox
believers, and in that sense of 'person', 'God' does not. 'God is
a mind or spirit, He thinks, He wills; but let us not humanize
Him – He does not think or will as we do.'[11] What He does is for
another chapter.

The argument I have offered is that there is Truth, that this
Truth can depend on nothing but itself for its existence, and is
the final explanation for any finite thing's existence. Whatever
shares in Being (whatever, by derivation, is) must have a single
explanation, which is what makes it one. Insofar as the cosmos
itself is one it is so by the omnipresence of an immaterial,
unextended, unlocalized necessity. That God exists, so far, is
just this statement: that there is something non-material and
infinite which is the final explanation for whatever is. Since it is
inescapably and clearly true that something is the case, we must
in the end conclude that there is something inescapable. There
can be no 'godless worlds', because for such imaginary worlds to
be real it would have to be true both that something was the case
and also that nothing was; both that they constitute intelligible
wholes and that there is no reason why they are precisely what
they are; both that they constitute intelligible wholes and that
there is no one principle at work throughout them.

But although I have defended the idea of 'necessary being'
against those who deny it, I have not done so in the usual context
of that denial. The 'ontological argument', so called, also
concludes that there is a Necessary Being: that than which
none greater can be conceived. The very idea of such perfection
demands that it be realized if possible.

To put the point another way: if there were no Being worthy
of the title 'God' (that is, that than which none greater can be
conceived), then there could not be. Not only could nothing
come into existence which would then deserve the title (for

nothing so ephemeral is unsurpassable), but there could be no other possible world where, for some reason, that God *did* exist. For any such merely possible being could also be surpassed (for a start, by all the similar beings that existed in more possible worlds than one). Its existence would also be contingent on some other feature of the world in question, and hence (as it were) be at its mercy. It follows that if there is no such Being then there couldn't be – and couldn't be precisely because its very concept prevents it. In brief, if God does not exist it can only be because the concept of 'God' makes it impossible. Conversely, if nothing in the concept of 'God' prevents God's real existence, then He does.

The argument is valid, but inconclusive, since it is apparently open to unbelievers to insist that there is, after all, some conceptual difficulty with the very concept of 'God' (as defined). My claim is that there isn't: there is nothing wrong, that is, with the concept of Infinite, Necessary Being, as what both unifies and explains all finite, and unnecessary beings. That than which none greater can be conceived can only be that Truth. The chief force of the ontological argument, however, is to make it clear that those who talk of God aren't speaking of any finite thing at all, nor something that exists in some possible worlds but not in all. It is therefore absurd to ask what difference there is between a possible world where God exists and one where He does not: there is no possible world where God does not – for 'being a possible world' is simply to be a state of affairs that God might realize, or the Truth explain. But we still need reason to believe that Being, Truth, God is 'perfect' in a sense demanding worship: what *is* it that a being than which none greater can be conceived must be, and why should we suppose that? The argument depends (as I observed in an earlier chapter) on our already 'knowing' what perfections are – but why should we not?

FIVE

HAVING THE MIND OF GOD

———

Intellect and Being

SUPPOSE I HAVE (as maybe I have not, since 'I am certainly aware of how many figments are born in the human heart, and what is my own heart but a human heart?')[1] established that there must be a real world, Truth, unlike my thought in being one, immaterial, infinite, necessary, and worth discovering. Why should we identify that Truth with anything the religious might call 'God'? What does it add to do so, and why did our predecessors think it obvious that what they had established is a perfect God's existence? A partial answer is already available: the Truth is understood to be worshipful even by those who deny that anything is to be worshipped. But more is usually expected of God than that: notably, that God has all 'perfections'. Might not a high-minded atheist respond that however worshipful we rightly conceive the Truth to be, it does not think or love or act? Either we should bow to the Truth even if it's ugly, boring, alien or frightful, or we shouldn't always bow, because it is these things. In either case it's not the only god.

Admittedly there have been theists, or professed theists, who have denied that God *does* think or love or act, or said that He does so only in some very distant sense. Any theist, like Malebranche, would agree that God's thought is not ours, but most would still suppose that there is at least a useful analogy between God's mode of being (so to speak) and ours, or that God is in some way more like us than like stones or trees or spiders, or at least as like us. Why should we suppose them right?

It is certain that there is Truth, or Being. It is almost as clear, Edwards said, that 'neither Can there be any such thing without consciousness. How is it possible there should something be from all Eternity and there be no consciousness of it. It will appear very Plain to every one that intensely Considers it that

Consciousness and being are the same exactly.'[2] We should not equate that Consciousness with our own. As Malebranche said:

> God is a mind or spirit, He thinks, He wills; but let us not humanize Him – He does not think or will as we do.... Rather we should believe that as He contains within Himself the perfections of matter without being material, since it is certain that matter is related to some perfection in God, so He also comprehends the perfections of created minds without being a mind in the way we conceive of minds, and that His true name is HE WHO IS, i.e. unrestricted being, all being, the infinite and universal being.'[3]

That Truth is the Light of which physical radiation is itself an image.

Some thinkers have found it obvious that we have no better model of the Truth than an infinite, free spirit, for we have no better notion of being than as *thinking* being. 'All agree that God is that thing which they place above all other things. And since all those who think of God think of something living, only they can think of Him without absurdity who think of Him as life itself.'[4] Augustine goes on to identify a better life with intelligent life, and then with immutable life: 'for a wise mind which has learned wisdom was not wise before it learned, but Wisdom itself was never foolish nor can be'. In this Augustine followed Aristotle: God *is* that life than which none better is conceivable.[5] Whatever Truth it is that transcends our thought, it can be nothing *less* than thought.

But precisely because our thought is fleeting, evanescent, submerged in an incessant chatter about this or that, we must also correct many implications of too 'literal' an interpretation of that image. This certainly creates difficulties. 'A mind whose acts and sentiments and ideas are not distinct and successive, one that is wholly simple and totally immutable, is a mind which has no thought, no reason, no will, no sentiment, no love, no hatred; or in a word no mind at all.'[6] Can there be *thought* where there can never be ignorance or uncertainty? Can there be *action* when just wishing makes it so? Those who think of God as a spiritual substance (in the sense of 'substance' and of 'spirit' that applies to us) make an error almost as great as those who think of Him as a corporeal one.[7]

The fact that we can be mistaken is proof that there is a fact of the matter, other than our thought of it. That very fact requires us to consider whether even our fondest thoughts are false, and whether what is 'obvious' may be illusion. If we are to reason rightly, there must be a right answer – but why does that require that Someone knows that answer, or even that Something 'knows' it, in a way? One answer is related to the argument of the earlier chapter: material existence does not itself account for unity. For there to be a single extended thing there must be something immaterial, unextended, present in it. For us to have good reason to believe that things far away and long ago are nonetheless united with our local samples we must also believe that Something is immaterially present everywhere – or that everything is present in It. What unifies the cosmos cannot simply be the universal presence of space–time, nor yet the travelling messengers we know as photons: both such alleged connectives are themselves stretched out, extended, things, and need some other unifying factor. Only an immaterial (an unextended) Unity suffices. Since 'matter' is characteristically opposed, at least in Cartesian circles, to 'mind', it may seem obvious that if matter is not itself the unifying factor, mind must be. But this is to assume too quickly that 'matter' and 'mind' exhaust the possibilities, and to run the risk (identified by Malebranche) of imputing far too many human features to the Unity. The argument must be more circumspect. As before, it turns on what we must acknowledge to be true if we are to believe that we can ever recognize the truth, or have good reasons for believing anything.

The Plotinian Argument

The last great pagan theist, Plotinus, argued as follows:

Since, then, there exists soul which reasons about what is right and good, and discursive reasoning which enquires about the rightness (*dikaion*) and goodness (*kalon*)[8] of this or that particular thing, there must be some further permanent rightness from which arises the discursive reasoning in the realm of soul. Or how else would it manage to reason? And if soul sometimes reasons about the right and good and sometimes does not, there must be in us Intellect which does not reason discursively but always possesses the right, and there must be also the principle and cause and God of Intellect. He is not divided, but abides, and as he does not abide in place he is contemplated in many beings, in each and every one of those capable of receiving him as another self, just as the centre of a circle exists by itself, but every one of the radii has its point in the centre and the lines bring their individuality to it. For it is with something of this sort in ourselves that we are in contact with God and are with him and depend upon him, and those of us who converge towards him are firmly established in him.[9]

The argument is compressed, but I believe it to be convincing. The question is: what is it of which one may rightly be convinced?

'Since we reason about the right and good, there must be something right from which such reasoning takes its start. How else would we manage to reason?' The first reading of this identifies the need, in any reasoning, for premises. If our premises are wrong, so will all our reasonings be. And where do we get right premises? What is the nature and beginning of that form of intellect which grasps right premises, without needing to reason its way toward them?

If we are to use the word in its true sense, we must take this intellect to be, not that in potentiality or that which passes from stupidity to intelligence – otherwise we shall have to look for another intellect before it – but that which is actually and always intellect. But if it does not have its thinking from outside, then if it thinks anything it has it from itself. But if it thinks from itself, it is itself what it thinks.[10]

We might conclude that Plotinus only intends an Aristotelian division between discursive and intuitive reason. We cannot suppose that everything we grasp as true is something that we have deduced from earlier knowledge: how then could there be an end to reasoning? Some premises are ones that are grasped as soon as they are seen (which is not to say that we always see them), without which we could not even start to reason. But the relevant, Aristotelian, division is more likely to be between 'active' and 'passive' intellect. We may recognize some premises as true as soon as we encounter them: until that moment we were unenlightened, and incapable of real reasoning. But what, without argument, we recognize as right was right before we recognized it. There must be 'some further permanent rightness' by which our reasonings are measured. If there were not (and our intuitive judgements, accordingly, were only what we do, where others might as reasonably do otherwise), there are no real premises nor any standards of 'right reasoning' outside our whim or biological fancy.

It has been fashionable to deplore 'foundationalism', the idea that there are axioms from which we might legitimately derive new knowledge, and without which we cannot think at all. That, it has been said, was the Cartesian error – to believe that we could get outside the framework of the House of Knowledge to inspect foundations. Far from being the axioms on which the House is raised, 'foundational truths' are only aspects of the architecture, and themselves dependent on the whole system, the context of all reasoning, beyond which there is nothing we can 'rightly' rely on. I shall address that aspect of the case in a later chapter, dealing with Prejudice and Tradition. For the moment all that is asserted is just this: if we are to reason rightly, or to think we could, we must acknowledge that there are right answers which transcend our thought of them. We must at the same time realize that those right answers cannot be separated from a right cognition. All that our cognition could then be, if they were separate, would be a mirroring of putative 'right answers' – but no one, precisely, could ever compare the truth with what we thought of it. The sceptical gap would open, irretrievably. 'If [Intellect and the intelligible] are not the same, there will not be truth':[11] which is, of course, absurd. Right answers precede our recognition of them, but the recognition itself must be identical with those right answers: accordingly they must be known before *we* know we know them, and our coming to know them is to be seen as the uncovering of an abiding knowledge.

Some will still ask why isn't it enough that certain conclusions *would* be drawn, if there were anyone to draw them (as certain sights or sounds would be perceived, if there were an observer)?

The answer is very simple: what guarantees that we *should* draw those conclusions, except the *fact* that they are already right? 'What else could calculation (*to logizesthai*) be but the effort to find intelligence (*phronesis*) and reason which is true and attains to the truly existent?'[12] That true reason, whether it is of wholly indemonstrable truths or of those truths which *we* need to demonstrate, is inseparable from its object. 'The knowledge of immaterial things is the same as its object.'[13] So when we reason our way to understanding of some truth (and so become wise) we must recognize both the prior existence of that truth and, correspondingly, the prior existence of the intellect that contains it. On the one hand, if the intelligibles have their being independently of their being grasped by intellect, the intellect itself only grasps *impressions* of the intelligibles, and so cannot affirm its own *knowledge* of them (on which, see below). On the other, if there were no intellectual grasp of the truths we acquire until we had acquired them, there could till then only, at best, have been a possibility that they would come into existence. But unless there are some real truths already, what could require us to recognize any particular truths, as of right? The fact that we recognize some truths as permanent demands upon our attention itself demands that we accept the permanence of the intellect in which they exist. 'Forms (such as *dikaiosune* and *sophrosune* and true knowledge) exist in the souls which are in us, and these are not images or likenesses of their Forms... but those very Forms themselves existing here in a different mode.... For the sense world is in one place, but the intelligible world is everywhere.'[14] Coming to know them can only be accepting them into our souls, or finding them there already. The knowledge of all necessary being must already be in us, as intellect, and in all things that are as their abiding pattern.

The best way of realizing the truth of this is to suppose the opposite. If there were no permanent intellect then the indemonstrable truths from which reason takes its start would themselves be no more than the habits of mind peculiar to our particular sort of creature. If there were no intellect then the implications of those truths would only be the ones that creatures of our kind habitually draw. In that case there would be no right answers, and strict reasoning would be impossible. Wittgenstein's doubts about the proper application of such rules as 'For a given

number n, add 2' demand that there is a right way to apply the
rule which cannot itself be given by rule: only if all possible
numbers are already arrayed so as to pick out the result of that
straightforward operation can there be a right way to do it. If
there isn't (or they aren't) then anything at all might be,
conventionally, the 'right way forward' (and so there would be
no right way). Only if it is already the case that any well-
described action is right or wrong can there be a right way to
apply whatever moral rule is picked. In no case can there be a
'right way' to reason unless there is an intellect which already
knows the truth. The truths it knows are not isolated theorems:
if they were, they could not be known (any more than we could
know p if we did not know that anything inconsistent with it
must be false). 'Intellect as a whole is all the Forms...as the
whole body of knowledge is all its theorems, but each theorem is
part of the whole, not as being spatially distinct, but as having its
particular power in the whole. The Intellect therefore is in itself,
and since it possesses itself in peace is everlasting fullness.'[15]

The two principles on which Plotinus here relies seem to be as
follows. First, the actual precedes the potential. Second, extension cannot itself create unity.

That the actual precedes the potential may seem strange:
surely, before anything actually is, it must be possible for it to
be? Before anything is understood, it must be understandable.
What we *could* understand, as being implied by prior knowledge
or as luminously self-evident, need not be understood already.
But the obstacle to this commonsensical conclusion is clear: what
actual truth makes inference correct? We cannot trust only to
what, formally speaking, *could* be inferred from prior principle,
since there must always be such prior principles, and also a
correct conclusion. This can only be possible if there are already
real truths, and ones immediately understood. 'The very being of
intellect is wisdom: it does not exist first and then become
wise.'[16]

If we are to reason rightly, there must be a right answer, and
one that is known as such. Such answers cannot be supposed to
lie 'outside the intellect', since 'they would be the true realities;
and on this supposition it will contemplate them without
possessing them, but will only get images of them.'[17] If intellect
(*nous*) were not the same as what it intuited (*ta noeta*), 'there will

be no truth; for the one who is trying to possess realities will possess an impression different from the realities, and this is not truth.'[18] But in that case how could we even articulate the thought that all our reasonings might miss the mark? If we could only hope to *agree* with the truth, and never actually possess it, how could we even know that we *agreed* with it, or know what was meant by 'it'? 'In Intellect there is also the real truth, which does not agree with something else, but with itself, and says nothing other than itself, but it is what it says and it says what it is.'[19]

Briefly, since we reason about right and wrong, there are right answers. Since there are right answers (and ones by which we can be enlightened) they already constitute an organized system of implication which can only be real insofar as it is not just understandable, but understood. Recognizing those right answers in ourselves, we are made one with intellect: the very same intellect (how could there be another?) that all others also serve. 'Intellect is our king. But we too are kings when we are in accord with it.'[20] There can be no *truths* if there is no actual truth.

Even if we were all to deny that 2 + 2 = 4, it does. But what sort of being could such an organized system have? As Plotinus insists, these theorems cannot be isolated, as though 2 + 2 might equal 4, yet 3 + 1 make 52 instead. The very notion of 'a truth' (that is, a proposition which implies other truths, and is incompatible with imaginable falsehoods) makes no sense outside an intellectual system which is, as it were, the shape of the intellect. But what can make a mathematical or a moral system thus united? Considered just as theorems they exist at particular points within a virtually extended world, but it is of the essence of 'extension' (as above) that every point in it is different from every other. Different points, or different theorems, are united in intellect. 'It is not then possible for the real beings to exist if Intellect is not actively at work, for ever working one thing after another and, we may say, wandering down every way and wandering in itself . . . But it is everywhere itself, so its wandering is an abiding one.'[21] The theorems exist as theorems because they are actually linked in the Intellect, or (equivalently) in the Truth.

Evolution and the Analogy of Being

So the third noble truth is that God can be known by persons, and that this knowledge must reside in an eternal, unaffected intellect which we have intermittently, but God is always. In coming to realize the Truth, there awakens in us (or we awake to its presence) a realization that the very realization of Truth is not something other than that Truth. The knowledge of God is God's knowledge. Knowing Being we know that it is known from everlasting.

Once again, consider the alternative. The Truth, as above, breaks inwards on our dreaming, but if it were wholly alien, wholly other, then there would be no common terms even between the world of our enlightened experience, and That. We could never really wake. If, on the other hand, we ever do know what is going on then there is a presented world, a world experienced in human terms, that is identical with the world that contains all human terms. Would it be enough that the human present and the trans-human be 'similar'? But how could such similarity be assessed without having both present, without there being a human present that actually was identical with the trans-human world, without one in whom the fullness of the Godhead dwelt bodily? 'If any, other than you were to inspire me,' said Augustine to his God, 'I do not believe that my words would be true, for you are the Truth, whereas every man is a liar, and for this reason he who utters falsehood is only uttering what is natural to him.'[22] On the other hand, 'it is really the nature of the soul to live in union with the Divine Ideas, and it depends upon them whenever it pronounces one thing to be better than another.'[23] Only by the presence in us of that Intellect (which is also the Divine Ideas) can we speak truth.

If 'persons' are really only minor products of a fundamentally non-personal Reality there can be no good reason to suppose that persons ever map Reality at all. Maybe our local visions aren't too 'misleading' (though even this does not establish that they're 'true'): the idea that we could ever expect to reach out to the World at Large is ludicrous. So if we are right to believe that (say) scientific enquiry does reveal Reality, we have good reason to believe that there is a connection, an identity, between Truth and the Mind. Moreover it must be possible for a finite

intelligence to embody truth. There must be at least one thing
with two natures (the finite and the infinite) if there is to be a real
possibility of our achieving truth.

What must the Truth be like, if we can know it? It must, as I
observed in the previous chapter, include real universals. The
spectral death of nominalism was answered by 'Aquinas in the
chair of Aristotle, taking all knowledge as his province; and tens
of thousands of lads, down to the lowest ranks of peasant and
serf, living in rags and on crusts about the great colleges, came to
listen to the scholastic philosophy.'[24] Nominalism, I should add,
is indeed a death: the claim that there are no real classes, that
there is nothing genuinely the *same* from one punctiform particular to the 'next', destroys all thought and language, as well as
all possibility of knowing natural laws. It is not even a doctrine
that can be coherently stated: to say that two pigs are only two
distinct particulars to which the *same word*, 'pig' is regularly
applied is at once ridiculous and incompatible with the very
dogma that it states (since the token utterances of 'pig' share
nothing real). The realization of what things have in common
was something, Chesterton said, at which the scholastics ex-
celled; the recognition of the particular, of portraiture rather
than iconography, was a later development, even if foresha-
dowed in St. Francis's particularism.[25] It is an error to forget
either – and of course, they are not at odds. On the contrary, the
kind of particularism that emphasizes the distinct being of
ordinary individuals depends on there being, for each such
individual, a unity manifested in diversity:

> Each mortal thing does one thing and the same:
> Deals out that being indoors each one dwells:
> Selves – goes itself; myself it speaks and spells,
> Crying 'what I do is me: for that I came'.[26]

'As Aquinas said, that *is* a given thing which performs the
operations of the thing; the thing does not, then, exist if the
relevant operations cannot exist.'[27]

Can there be a world in which there is pattern but no
intelligence? Pattern exists when the *same* is present many
times over: but what sort of being has that *same*? Maybe
particulars can exist even without being noticed, but can a

pattern, a *same*, exist without being noticed? Can there be real universals not identified as such in an intelligence? If there are patterns in the world itself, and not simply in our deluded fantasy, then there is already something like a Mind in Reality, even before 'we' came to be. In fact that Mind truly deserves the title, more than we do: we have 'minds' only in that we are sometimes able to glimpse the patterns of the Real Mind expressing itself in Truth. That there are patterns depends on there being Mind;[28] that there is a unity (that the world actually is a cosmos rather than a muddle or an unintelligible heap) depends on Mind. The merely physical, or spatial, is of its nature spread out and disunited: nothing spatio-physical can unite the whole. That latter is done, as the last great pagan philosopher Plotinus said, by Soul and Intellect.

The Emergence of Conscious Being

Is God more like us than like stones, or trees, or frogs? Or is it enough to say that He is as much like us as them? It has seemed obvious to most theistical philosophers that beings can have no properties denied to Being. Whatever powers the beings have must be derived from Being (where else?). Plotinus (as so often) offered the most well-thought-out of those arguments.[29] The Soul, in particular, cannot be put together from unsouled parts. It seems clear to me that he was right in this. Two fashionable schools deny the implication, but only by adopting wilfully obscure and damaging devices.

The first such school denies that 'soul' is real: it is only, they say, a fiction to suppose that we are sentient. Our own sense of being, our feelings, meanings, or perceptions, are only physical events, of the same sort as elementary tropisms. Whereas Cartesians supposed that 'animals' were mechanisms but that we were minds, the modern school imagines that we are all 'animals' together – or rather that nothing happens but the physically describable, physically determined, biochemical reaction. We no more need to suppose the existence of real selves to govern our bodily movements than we need to suppose real angels to regulate planetary motions, or real flower fairies. 'The melancholy long withdrawing roar' of animistic sympathy has finally uncovered the dull pebbles which determine human life as well as animal, plant and geological 'behaviour'. Nothing ever 'really' happens but the motion of punctiform particulars according to general laws that nobody can state. No schoolman has yet convincingly shown that we can think of ourselves like this: that we can think of others, human or otherwise, like that is evident. Generally those who think of other humans so are identified as damaged, and as dangerous. Those who think, or purport to think, of 'animals' like that may be rewarded: an entire profession of animal experimentalists has chosen to believe – because it is convenient – that 'animals' are only stuff. The attempt, however unsuccesful, to think of ourselves in this way is at least 'consistent' – except of course that it is self-refuting (by any plausible standard) to insist that we don't think at all, while also demanding that we think of ourselves like that. Haldane's definition of 'materialism', as 'the view that all occurrences depend on phenomena obeying definite mathematical laws, which it is the business of physics to discover,'[30] contains the contradiction: hard materialists must in the end deny that there are *phenomena* at all, and that *physicists* have any business.

The second school is at least more rational in admitting that we really think. Their difficulty lies in explaining how such real thoughts, such real selves, are possible. It is supposed that at a certain level of 'complexity' of parts, new levels of description are appropriate because new entities 'emerge'. The 'emergent' properties of a whole are ones that cannot be grasped as mathematical transformations of properties possessed by the constituent parts. Science fantasists suggest that a telephone exchange (or else the Internet) could itself become so 'complex' that a real, governing unity would arise as something more than an appearance. The appearance of unity of course need not be very surprising: even starlight, branches and a passing bird can momentarily look much like a human face. That it would actually *be* a human face is more difficult for most of us to believe. Emergence amounts to just the sort of magic that rational realists rejected: 'write the runes just so, and for no reason anyone could see a demon will appear'; 'make the connections just so, and the computer network will, for no good reason, suddenly *be* a person'. But either what that 'person' does is only and entirely what the bits would do, or it is not: if it is, then nothing 'really' has emerged at all (and the second school is the same as the first); if it isn't, then there is something real in addition to anything that physics can describe, let alone explain.

There are in essence three positions only: there are no selves, nor any conscious being; there are selves, minds, feelings, meanings, but these 'emerge' for no clear reason on the back of merely physical events, and without any reason to believe they replicate or mirror 'the real world'; there are indeed real selves, themselves the source of unity in the material beings we identify as bodies. The second position, so it seems, dissolves into the first or third. The first is literally incredible. Accordingly, it is only the third position that is worth advancing. So far from explaining 'soul' by physics, we should attempt to explain physics by reference to soul. 'Physics', after all, was originally the study of what happened 'by nature' (*phusis*): that is, of itself. 'Soul', on the other hand, was what moved itself. Physics was from its beginning all about such soul.

Anti-realists are correct at least in this, that the world of our very own experience is unified in that experience: what conflicts with our chosen sense of who and what we are is either forgotten or fenced off. The realization of a wider world – in the end, of an infinitely wider world – is something that we often resist, preferring to sink back into our dreams. Insofar as we admit that real existence, of a real world that does not depend on us and on what we may say of it, we need to understand how that real world is unified itself. If it can't be unified it remains mere chaos, something at the fringes of our own significant world: if it comes across to us as more than that – and it is implicit in everything I have said so far that it must be more than that – it is as the world of an infinite intellect. The world's being, and unity, can only rest in a principle that is itself alive, and thinking. The real world, we might say, a little misleadingly, is what God dreams. God, by hypothesis, 'imagines' the cosmos into being, and the being it has is never opaque to Him: it is nothing but what He imagines it as being (which is why Berkeley was correct to see that theism entails the non-existence of a strictly material world).[31]

The universe can be considered both as 'all the things there are' and 'everything that is the case'. The former conception sometimes leads commentators to adopt a fully materialist view. The second is associated with idealism, on the grounds that 'being the case' can only be 'being counted as true by someone capable of providing such descriptions'. Others have held, as plausibly, that being 'a thing' is just as much dependent on marks, descriptions, implications. Too strong a dose of such idealism leads to anti-realism, to the conviction that we change the world itself by redescribing it. Too strong a dose of materialism must in the end make it impossible to see how we can ever get things right, or even ourselves be real. Theism rests in the conviction that there is a unified real world, the world that is descried in God. The world is real, and a real unity, because it exists in Someone, who both understands and feels it.

The Context of Being

If the world is unified through the Omnipresence of Necessary Being, which serves as a universal, stable explanation of whatever happens, then that thing contains, implicitly, the patterns or laws which mediate that explanation. Those patterns themselves can only be unified, as theorems of a single system, through the operation of Intellect. Intellect, considered as a complete system, is still, according to Plotinus, less than the real source of unity, just in that there is an implicit duality between the thoughts and the thinking which together constitute Intellect and Intelligibles. The eternal Intellect itself exists because of the first principle, the One. There is also a third: whereas the eternal Intellect, by its nature, knows all things together (equivalently, every thing that's known is simultaneously present to It, without any shadow or obscurity), we must also agree that things are present successively. There is, it is evident, a form of life distinguishing past, present and future. Even if what's happening here and now is known, in its essentials, from eternity, there is still a sense in which it is known *now*. In Plotinus's development of the Platonic tradition, Soul experiences sequentially, and from many different perspectives: the world of soul (our world) exists because the world of intellect (to which we can aspire) exists eternally, and that in turn because of the One, the root of every finite existent.

The Plotinian Trinity has genuinely Platonic roots (though it is not now clear quite what Plato himself intended). It also apes or mirrors or explains the Christian Trinity. My present task, however, is not to compare or to contrast those trinitarian conceptions, but to reason my way to Truth, so far as this is possible. What can be said to support a strong analogy between the Truth and Soul? Might not the Truth, even the Truth of Intellect, be as impersonal as Spinoza thought? Might there be as little resemblance between the Mind of God and ours as between the Dog-Star and a dog?

The question is: how is there Soul at all? I have offered Plotinian reasons for suspecting that a putatively 'soul-less' aggregate cannot, in reason, generate a soul. On the contrary, the aggregate itself exists as something more than a heap because of soul, and so indeed do all component parts, themselves in need of unity. But more can be said: all the things there are (or seem to be) present themselves within the soul. As Plotinus also said: without the soul (that is, without conscious being) there is nothing. How can we claim to talk of what transcends experience: the merely material? We know of that only (at best) by our extrapolation. Our only model of being is presence. It is only within presence that anything exists at all. Plotinus again:

> This is how soul should reason about the manner in which it grants life to the whole universe and in individual things. Let it look at the great soul, being itself another soul which is no small one, which has become worthy to look by being freed from deceit and the things that have bewitched the other souls, and is established in quietude. Let not only its encompassing body and the body's raging sea be quiet, but all its environment: the earth quiet, and the sea and air quiet, and the heaven itself at peace. Into this heaven at rest let it imagine soul as if flowing in from outside, pouring in and entering it everywhere and illuminating it: as the rays of the sun light up a dark cloud, and make it shine and give it a golden look, so soul entering into the body of heaven gives it life and gives it immortality and wakes what lies inert. And heaven, moved with an everlasting motion by the wise guidance of soul, becomes a fortunate living being, and gains its value by the indwelling of soul; before soul it was a dead body, earth and

water; or rather the darkness of matter and non-existence . . .[32]

Soul Itself, 'which never departs from itself,'[33] is eternal: its presence in individual bodies, and in the whole material cosmos, is what gives those bodies their reality. If there were somewhere a working cosmos without soul (*per incredibile*) there would be no strictly temporal distinctions there, any more than any part of it would be uniquely 'here'. The image Plotinus offers may seem to suggest that bodies (or at least material stuff or spatial extension) exist, unknown, before they are illuminated: but this is no more than a manner of speaking. Without soul, they are nothing. The soul which makes the cosmos one, by Plotinus's account, is our sister, not our mother: Soul itself, multiply refracted or reflected in the world of time, is that of which succession is an image.

Look at it another way: the cosmos, I have said before, is unified by the presence everywhere in it of Intellect, conceived itself as the union of Forms in a single, coherent system. But Intellect (as we conceive it) may have limits: what it grasps is only what is graspable by intellect. Even the Divine Intellect may not, of itself, be able to contain mere happenstance. As some philosophical theists have suggested, God may know the laws but not the infinite particulars, insofar as they are not determined by the laws. If everything were fixed by abstract law then God would indeed know everything as fixed. If there is instead a level of random variation, not fixed by law, then God's knowledge of the law does not guarantee He knows it. If, on the other hand, we must suppose that everything, however fluid or unfixed, still rests upon God's Being, there must be some way of conceiving God's acquaintance with it. Soul, as distinct from Intellect, suffices: God's knowledge of everything need not be only intellectual. The Omnipresence of Necessary Being, if it is to be really omnipresent, must also be conceived as Soul.

Part of the problem about 'emergence' lies in our construction of a 'real world' outwith all sentient experience. Realizing that experience differs, that what feels warm to one feels cold to another (and so throughout the other sensory modalities), we choose to concentrate on those features of the world that we can suppose 'objective'. Maybe warmth and colour, subjectively conceived, are functions of the observing mind, but size, shape, structure (and the rest) are more objective. 'The world itself', we tell ourselves, is made of 'atoms and the void' (all else is by agreement). Having posited that world on the far side of all possible experience we are confronted by the problem, where experience came from. By hypothesis, the 'objective' world is one that has no 'merely subjective' properties, nor any from which they could be mathematically derived. Absurdly, having decided to suppose that feelings, colours and the rest are only 'mental projections' on an unconscious universe, we end by either supposing that conscious being is an alien intruder without any direct grasp of that 'objective' being, or that consciousness itself is 'a projection'. Either our experience is never more than a dream which might or might not 'mirror' an objective world, or else we don't experience at all (which is absurd). It seems easier, and more fruitful, to reject the original experiment by which we constructed an 'objective world' whose properties are not those of the experienced world. According to objectivists 'the Wall is not white, Fire is not hot & c. We Irishmen', said Berkeley ironically, 'cannot attain to these truths.'[34]

If we are to think that our own sentient being is an intelligible part of the cosmos, and that we have some chance of uncovering other aspects of that cosmos (as not being utterly alien to us), we must suppose that 'Soul' can reach out everywhere because it's there already. Malebranche uses as an argument against the imputation of secondary qualities to the things themselves that if they were in the objects, our souls would reach out to the heavens ('it seems to me beyond question that our souls do not occupy a space so vast as that between us and the fixed stars ... thus, it is unreasonable to think that our souls are in the heavens when they see stars there').[35] But Herbert's mystical rationalism concluded that our souls *could* reach out even to the stars, and far beyond:

> When you have left the womb of the lower world, will you not attain to what you formerly conceived as ideal? On this journey you will first encounter the blue which is commonly supposed to be the ceiling of heaven; but this is ignorance. For in reality it consists of the most refined region of the air which appears to be this colour owing to its distance, as experts in

optics tell us. When you have passed through this tract you will discover the stars to have been created not merely to sparkle but to be new worlds. And at last, to prolong the account no further, the infinite itself will unfold.[36]

What really would be absurd would be to suppose that the worlds beyond will be created when we come to see them: what we discover is uncovered only. A similar argument concerns those evolutionary ages before, so we are told, there were living creatures capable of experiencing the world as we do. It is easy to imagine that there were such ages: what is difficult is giving any adequate account of them. Once again, if we divide the 'subjective' from the 'objective' world we cannot simultaneously claim that there were objects of the present kind 'back then'. What living worlds existed then, what shapes carved from the Uncarved Block, who knows? No doubt God has His views – which we should not think are just like ours (as though the Truth was waiting for us, and we know it all). The Truth is: we don't know, but hope for more.

SIX

THE BEAUTIFUL AND TRUE

The Road to Beauty

THE GOD DEPICTED in my argument so far is the one immaterial and omnipresent principle on which all beings depend, which eternally contains (not as in an extended space, but somewhat as we 'contain' our thoughts) the forms of being, and is the field within which all experience takes shape. The path of true philosophy is to seek to see 'as God sees' (though we know our sight can never be so extensive). We recognize that Truth as worth acknowledging and waking up to even if it turned out ugly, alien or frightful – but there may be reason to suspect it won't. Even if everything happened in accordance with mathematically derivable laws such that thoughts and feelings were no more than transformations of material size and shape (which is absurd), those mathematical laws themselves would be a form of beauty.

There are those who believe that human intelligence is something quite unlike anything to be found 'in nature'. Strangely, few of them suppose that there is any other world from which 'intelligence' descends, or seem to realise the problem of explaining how such an alien, but weirdly effective, power could ever have emerged from nature. That issue is one that I address a little later. For the moment, I wish to draw attention to the presence of 'intelligence' (even if it is not a *human* intelligence) in nature. My argument, initially, will make no reference to any of the 'anti-naturalist' conclusions I have reached so far.

Engineers, notoriously, may learn a trick or two from seeing how animals or plants have coped with engineering problems. One random example: Etrich and Wells' 1904 glider is copied from the seed of *Zanonia macrocarpa*.[1] The techniques forged by natural selection may be essential information for the environmentally conscious engineer. They are, after all, the ones that have survived so far. It is conceivable that human

engineering skills should produce better and more elegant
solutions (human beings have invented wheeled transport, for
example, though there are probably good reasons for living
creatures not to have attempted quite that technique), but we
have good reason to try out the older methods first. Paturi, from
whom I drew the example of the *Zanonia* glider, argues that our
aesthetic sense, our recognition of good proportion, is 'developed, disciplined and enlivened' by our natural environment.[2]
The proportions that we find aesthetically pleasing are the ones
that are found in healthy organisms (especially plants). Paturi
claims, for example, that the Golden Section (a particularly
pleasing proportion of 21 to 34) is to be found throughout
plant architecture, 'not certainly from any aesthetic feeling, but
from pure reasons of expediency'.[3] How far this is true I do not
know, though there seems nothing impossible about it. The
research on which Paturi's claim is based, namely Fechner's, is
disputed by Valentine,[4] but it is still very likely both that our
aesthetic judgement is grounded in our biology, and that it is
developed by living in 'natural' environments.

Our ancestors have had good reason to be aware of, and to be
attracted by, what is healthy and well-proportioned. What we
appreciate in such health and sound proportion is beauty; the
evolutionary explanation of our having such tastes is that what
is beautiful is also soundly engineered. That is not to conclude
that what we ought to value was what we recognized as sound
engineering. That would be a fallacy for many reasons: first, that
what we actually value is the well-proportioned, not the
economically useful engineering. The fact that what is well-
proportioned is also soundly constructed may help to explain
why we have this taste; it does not prove that we value beauty
only insofar as we see that it is economically useful, any more
than people value beauty in each other merely as an outward
sign of good health and equable temperament, let alone a
healthy bank balance. The evolutionary explanation of their
valuing it does not provide them with an additional motive for
doing so; still less does it prove that they do not really value it as
inherently admirable, or that they have the most superficial and
philistine of goals in mind.

Second, even if we agreed that engineering efficiency was what
we were looking for, under the guise of good proportion, it

would still be unwise to put aside our aesthetic sense in favour of new-fangled calculation of efficiency. There is good reason to suspect that a healthy organism's immediate response to the situation is more reliable than calculation. If one's grasp of what is beautiful and what is not accepts one building as better proportioned than another, it is probable that it really is a sounder construction, even if the architect and builder were only trusting their eyes in building it. The architect who claims to have 'proved' that her building is better, though it looks a mess, may reasonably be distrusted (though not perhaps for ever – maybe our eyes will adjust in the end). This may also serve to explain Hermann Weyl's apparently shocking claim that he had 'always tried to unite the true with the beautiful; but when [he] had to choose one or the other, [he] usually chose the beautiful'.[5] A great scientist's educated sensibility is sometimes more reliable than what can – at the time – be demonstrated to less subtle wits.

A third reason for thinking that it would be wrong simply to substitute engineering efficiency for aesthetic proportion in our judgement on new constructions runs as follows. Even if we agreed to value beauty only as a clue to what was 'really valuable' (which is not what we do now), and even if we were convinced that precise mathematical calculation of structural efficiency were going to be more accurate than the educated eye in picking out what would be efficient, we should still resist 'philistinism'. The philistine wishes us to believe that efficiency is all that matters to us: but efficiency is, essentially, instrumentalist. Things can only be efficient for definite ends: the seed of *Zanonia macrocarpa* is an efficient glider, but a lousy hammer. The philistine transforms all things into tools, but leaves herself no goal in terms of which such instrumental efficiency can be calculated except sensual pleasure or the feeling of power over others. Even if we do agree that beauty is only derivatively valuable, as a means or as a clue, we shall need to insist that some things are non-derivatively valuable, and incidentally that mere survival or gene-reduplication are not among them.

There is a fourth reason: that 'efficient' buildings, even if beautiful, usually only embody some relatively simple, static structure. 'Why is it that the silhouette of a storm-bent leafless tree against an evening sky in winter is perceived as beautiful, but the corresponding silhouette of any multi-purpose university building is not, in spite of all efforts of the architect? The answer seems to me, even if somewhat speculatively,' said Eilenberger,[6] 'to follow from the new insights into dynamical systems. Our feeling for beauty is inspired by the harmonious arrangement of order and disorder as it occurs in natural objects – in clouds, trees, mountain ranges, or snow crystals. The shapes of all these are dynamical processes jelled into physical forms, and particular combinations of order and disorder are typical for them.' But Eilenberger was not being all that original. The ancient, 'classical' belief that beauty resides in proportion and appropriate size[7] is usually contrasted with the romantic view that beauty is a matter of exuberant vitality, incorporating some element of what – at an instant – seems disordered. When properly understood these views are not so different.

Thomas Burnet (c.1635–1715), in his *Sacred History*, conceived that the one original world was sternly geometrical, and that its present ragged edges and air of disorder is the relic of a prehistoric catastrophe. But even if there is a truth hidden in the thought that, as Chesterton put it, 'all good [is] a remnant to be stored and held sacred out of some primordial ruin,'[8] it is naive to think that such simple, static geometrical shapes as circle and square define the truly beautiful. True beauty, for Plotinus, lies in life, that marvellous, seemingly chaotic tangle that has – for us – its being over time. The patterns of the Mandelbrot set strike us as enthrallingly beautiful precisely because they are infinitely various, and always new, and yet identifiably the same. In Plotinus's words:

> For why is there more light of beauty on a living face and only a trace of it on a dead one, even if its flesh and proportions are not yet wasted away? And are not statues more beautiful if they are more lifelike, even if others are better proportioned; and is not an ugly living man more beautiful than a beautiful statue?[9]

Moral Beauty

That 'beautiful' is something more than what we call those things that give us a particular sort of thrill may be difficult to establish. Modern subjectivists or anti-realists are especially hard to convince – partly, no doubt, because they can admit no objective rational obligation to be convinced of anything. But it does not seem unreasonable to speak of 'the beautiful' as that feature which our evolution and our history have made us see as inherently valuable, and which is generally an accurate guide to the health and sound proportion of the thing (which includes its characteristic activity, and is likely to be far more complex than Burnet imagined). That moral approbation comes under the same heading is a thought that has been out of fashion for many years.[10] We have so far forgotten our past as to imagine that calling a character beautiful is only a strained metaphor. But we can at least understand what Plotinus means:

> As it is not for those to speak of the graceful forms of the material world who have never seen them or known their grace – men born blind, let us suppose – in the same way those must be silent upon the beauty of noble conduct and of learning and all that order who have never cared for such things, nor may those tell of the splendour of virtue who have never known the face of Justice and of Moral Wisdom beautiful beyond the beauty of Evening and Dawn. Such vision is for those only who see with the Soul's sight – and at the vision they will rejoice, and awe will fall upon them and a trouble deeper than all the rest could ever stir, for now they are moving in the realm of Truth. This is the spirit that Beauty must ever induce, wonderment and a delicious trouble, longing and love and a trembling that is all delight.[11]

Beauty, in brief, has in the past been reckoned not merely analogous to Moral Worth: it is what Moral Worth consists in, the beauty of action and the virtuous soul, the sight of which induces 'wonderment and a delicious trouble'. 'The equivalence of moral beauty and the good was a conception inherited from the Stoics, from Cicero and from Augustine, very likely from Aristotle's *Rhetoric* (1366a33) as well.'[12] If that is not how most of us feel about morality, so much the worse for us. The beauty that is evident in bodily form and movement is something that we have evolved to appreciate, for the sort of reasons that I have already sketched. The same may be true of the beauty evident in virtuous action and character: that is to say, those organisms which were moved to respect, love, imitate certain kinds of character and behaviour left more descendants than those that were not. They were not moved by the thought that they would leave more descendants: they could not, in general, have made that calculation, and would in any case be unlikely to reckon that outcome amongst their goals. If anyone does care whether more people in the year Three Million resemble her than her sister or her neighbour or an anonymous bushman, is that not because she wants the things she values still to be cared for (and foolishly imagines that her own descendants will be more like her)? It may be, nonetheless, that the values we bring to our decision-making are the ones that, in the past, have served to multiply our own ancestors' genes rather than those of our ancestors' contemporaries, who found their delights elsewhere. That may be the explanation (or one explanation) for why we have the values that we do: it does not constitute a justification of those values, as if they were valuable to us only as means to the survival of the 'the selfish gene'.

But let me return to an earlier stage of the argument. We have evolved, and been conditioned (so it's said), to appreciate just those forms that are generally symptomatic of good order. Since what we value is the aesthetically pleasing we can, in a sense, be tricked: cosmetics and hair-sprays can give us the impression of 'natural beauty', which is a symptom of good health; physical gracefulness can give us the impression of 'natural nobility', which is a symptom of what is fittest in mate or co-parent – a good deal of animal sexual display is bluff. Faced by this problem we may decide that we ought not to let ourselves be 'deceived', that there is a beauty that is more than skin-deep, a value that rests in being an honest and loyal friend. 'Interior beauty is more comely than external ornament, more even than the pomp of kings.'[13] We may also decide to go on valuing artificial beauty, and to look no deeper:

> Some look to see the sweet Outlines
> And beauteous Forms that Love does wear.
> Some look to find out Patches, Paint,
> Bracelets & Stays & Powder'd Hair.[14]

Natural selection has produced many ways of solving the sort of engineering problems that humans too may face. It has also produced many ways of solving social and personal problems, problems about how to organize one's life, and how to co-operate with others. But the creatures concerned cannot usually be supposed to have it in mind to solve these problems, and what attracts them in the direction they must go is not the thought of a solution. They do things because, at the time, they want to, and what they want to do is usually what they need to want to do if their kind of creature is going to survive. Animals do not court and mate in order to have offspring. We, who can conceive of having offspring and of acting towards that goal, can also take steps to mate and not have any offspring.

At this point in the argument it is usual to say that our goals are not determined by our biology. What we choose to value need not be what has guided natural selection (namely, the differential reproduction of genes), nor need it be what natural selection has caused us to desire (namely, sweet foods and sexy bodies and the affection of our peers). I am myself quite happy to agree that our desires and our rational evaluations are just what might be expected of a placental mammal with a lengthy infancy, sexual dimorphism, and the gift of the gab. This is not inconsistent with the thought that we are that sort of placental mammal because we were intended to be rational lovers of the good, the beautiful and true. In that sense our biology does 'determine' our morality, although (in the absence of decent control experiments) we shall probably never be sure quite how:

> It seems in a high degree probable...that any animal what-ever, endowed with well-marked social instincts, the parental and filial affections being here included, would inevitably acquire a moral sense or conscience, as soon as his intellectual powers had become as well developed, or nearly as well developed, as in man....I do not wish to maintain that any strictly social animal, if its intellectual faculties were to become as active and as highly developed as in man, would acquire exactly the same moral sense as ours.[15]

How far it is true that all human beings have 'the same moral sense' is itself a moot point (and one that Darwin's own – fashionably contemptuous – account of 'the immorality of savages' rebuts).[16] But I am willing to conceive either that they do (in the sense that all normal humans value friendship, resent disloyalty, and seek to guide their conduct by some image of the good society that incorporates worthwhile and enjoyable roles), or that they do not (and that differences between human populations in this respect might in theory be explained by sociobiological investigation – though I know of no convincing example of such explanation, Tibetan polyandries notwithstanding). The explanation of our having the morality, or the moralities, we do may well include some reference to the inclusive genetic fitness of those who operate by such standards. Courage, courtesy, chastity, temperance, prudence, generosity, proper pride, loyalty and justice are all sound Aristotelian virtues over all the world (although they may be manifested in different behaviour in widely differing circumstances). Such virtues, very likely, are the ones that, by and large, we must still have if we are going to leave descendants. Treacherous cowards, disloyal and penny-pinching scoundrels, who can control neither their lusts nor their ill-temper, may win an occasional advantage, but not the game. The virtuous do not act in order to win the game, and are not much troubled if they sometimes lose: that is why they win.

Vice is not so much an evolutionary disadvantage as to have been eliminated from the race, but any advantages a vice may win it wins because there is a virtue rather like it. Just as sickle-cell anaemia remains to trouble us because the heterozygotic form of that genome provides immunity to malaria (though the homozygotic form produces sickle-cell anaemia), so vice constantly returns because associated virtues are so much an evolutionary advantage. Courage becomes madness, courtesy cowardice; generosity and proper pride may turn to arrogant prodigality. As Thucydides noted:

> Words change their ordinary meanings and [are] construed in new senses. Reckless daring passe[s] for the courage of a loyal partisan, far-sighted hesitation [is] the excuse of a coward, moderation [is] the pretext of the unmanly, the power to see all sides of a question [is] complete inability to act. Impulsive rashness [is] held the mark of a man, caution in conspiracy [is] a specious excuse for avoiding action.[17]

As Aristotle argued, even virtues need to be balanced by their virtuous opposites: true and complete virtue lies in – living – proportion. By this account there will be a human norm, as there are also wolf or dolphin norms. 'Not for the human race only, but for every race, there are laws of right living. Given its environment, and its structure, there is for each kind of creature a set of actions adapted in their kinds, amounts and combinations to secure the highest conservation its nature permits.'[18] We can expect that virtue (as I have roughly described it) will prevail, in the sense that too great a departure from the human norm in any human population is likely to eliminate itself over the long run. Most human beings, accident and illness and corrupt manners permitting, will be fairly healthy and fairly virtuous.

Such a fairly healthy and fairly virtuous people would, and do, find that 'natural goods' are indeed good for them.[19] Natural goods are those things that people will, by and large, desire: honour and wealth and bodily strength and friendship and good fortune. Such things, by and large, will assist their fond possessor to survive, and to reproduce her kind; but they will only do harm to one who is cowardly, discourteous and depraved. If one is temperamentally villainous it would be better for one not to rise to power in a State, not to have the chance of acting out one's depraved passions. What is good in the abstract, what any reasonable person would prefer to have than not to have, will be good for the good person, but not for the bad, since the bad person will make ill use even of such excellences as she has. Vigorous villains will be worse off than lazy ones, especially if rich.

But none of this, even if it is true, gives us what traditionalists (like me) require. Maybe our line, to last, must cultivate those virtues: but should our line last? Or could it alter, over evolutionary aeons, into something rather different without real loss? Fashions in physical beauty change: why may not fashions in the deeper beauty? Some of our descendants may yet be supermantises, or sea-squirts,[20] and their virtues will not be ours. Darwin himself insisted that 'if men were reared under precisely the same conditions as hive-bees, there can hardly be a doubt that our unmarried females would...think it a sacred duty to kill their brothers, and mothers would strive to kill their fertile daughters; and no one would think of interfering'.[21]

A merely naturalistic account of who and what we are must identify old notions of Moral Beauty as errors, and I have yet to see any plausible reconstruction of traditional morality without those notions.[22] Darwin's praise of Duty,[23] or the righteousness of being kind to animals,[24] cannot long survive the conviction that we have the feelings that we do for socio-historical causes having nothing to do with any real Moral Beauty. Nor can one long maintain Darwin's confident rejection of the 'senseless customs' and superstitions of other varieties of humankind. 'Social Darwinists' chose to emphasize, mistakenly, the importance for our line of successful, even aggressive, competition. 'Sociable Darwinists', so to call them, prefer to draw attention to the genetic advantages of courteous co-operation – but even those rules of conduct are, by sound religious standards, only nepotistic and worldly minded. The call of duty, or of beauty, goes beyond.

Perfect virtue is complete virtue, with every disposition well-proportioned, and the goal of action Beauty. Truly virtuous people, according to tradition, do not merely recognize natural goods as being good-for-them, and act accordingly. They act for the sake of the beautiful – not, that is, to benefit the beautiful, but to exemplify it, to give it an entry to the changing world. They act so as to be performing beautifully, whether their act must be to deal with ill-health and poverty, or with the natural goods.[25] Perfectly virtuous people act so as to embody in their character and conduct the ideal of sound, and lively, proportion that our evolution has constrained us to intuit, the beauty that Plotinus praised so largely. This, traditionally, has been the ethical ideal: not simply to secure what is good-for-oneself as a healthy and harmonious human being, things like honour and friendship and a quiet life, but to do what is fine and noble, what is objectively required not simply for the good of the agent, but for the beauty of the act itself.

Such morality, putting oneself at the service of the beautiful, Aristotle seems to equate with service and contemplation of the god,[26] which is known in those who are themselves good-and-beautiful, and in the order and proportion of the heavens and of living things. If Aristotle is correct then it is not only true that our morality is founded on our biology (our perception of what is right and good upon the consequences of such perception for our evolutionary success). Our biology is founded on 'morality', on the pattern of due order and consequence by which all things are governed. 'The plant is not in love with the Fibonacci series [which describe its stalk-production]; it does not seek beauty through the use of the golden section; it does not even count its stalks; it just puts out stalks where they will have the most room.'[27] But the order it unfolds or reveals is undoubtedly a real and powerful one, that is made known to us as beauty. It is because the beautiful is what it is that bees must build their combs just so, if they are to live as bees. It is because the beautiful is what it is that human beings must have the desires and values that they do. Because there is order and living proportion in the universe, because all things strive to maintain their own being after their own kind, human beings must learn to find their own place in the cosmic order. In this, we are all moved by love: what is it, after all, for the plant to 'love' the Fibonacci series except that it is moved to live that way? What is it to love God if not to do justice and love mercy?

The delicious trouble that is the awakening of love, so Plato suggested, marked the budding of our wings. Once again, the flight of birds has been used to evoke that sense of liberation which is a key to faith. We are called out of our comfortable houses by the promise (perhaps it is literally a promise) of beauty.

Naturalistic Explanation

If our aesthetic, and our moral, sense is to be anything more than an adaptive (or sometime adaptive) trait, we must suppose that there is an objective Beauty which has causal importance in the way things work. That claim is not implausible. Great scientists frequently acknowledge how significant it is that theories should be 'beautiful'. Nothing that a sociobiologist could say or discover would establish that it is *not* the case that our evolution has brought us to the point of being able to see and appreciate and act so as to secure an objective beauty in the universe and in the character and actions of the virtuous. Our morality is founded on our biology in one sense, just as our science is founded on our biology: creatures of other imaginable biological natures might have very different ways of perceiving the world, and (for all we know) quite different ways of explaining it. Such creatures and ourselves, if scientific realism has anything going for it, could come to some agreement about what was the true account of how things happen. If moral realism is correct, we could also come to some agreement about what would be objectively beautiful. If the contrary hypothesis is preferred, that we could not expect agreement on what ought to be, it is difficult to see how we could expect agreement on what was. By hypothesis such aliens would not care whether what they said was 'appropriate' or 'mathematically elegant'. No moral realism means no scientific realism either. Astronomy would be no more than 'a complicated description of part of the course of human and possibly animal sensation'.[28]

This is not intended to conclude the argument. Realism about the Good and Beautiful has its difficulties, and the argument I have just given could be rebutted. I can also agree with McDowell[29] that the notion of 'objectivity' that seems so obvious to some commentators is deeply obscure (and – as I argued in the last chapter – makes our actual experience unintelligible). What world is it that might or might not have moral and aesthetic value 'in its fabric'? The world we live in as humans, as mammals, indubitably does: we can have no conception of a world fit for humans, or for mammals, that is not deeply structured by such values. The world-apart-from-value is a theoretical construct, devised for political purposes quite as much as for 'scientific', and not obviously the only really-real world. Where I differ from McDowell and similar anti-realists is in accepting that causal precedence defines the real: if moral and aesthetic values really had no influence on the world they would indeed be no true part of the real. But the truth to which great scientists have testified is that Beauty is indeed their firmest guide to truth: 'it is indeed an incredible fact that what the human mind, at its best and most profound, perceives as beautiful finds its realization in external nature.'[30] My own conclusion is that the Beautiful is indeed a constraint on what can happen, and that natural selection and engineering efficiency have generated – because so they were intended – creatures that can look directly toward the Beautiful, and not merely at its reflection and shadow, natural good.

In brief: if there were no real Beauty, nothing to constrain the shifting forms which matter can assume, and nothing to guide our view of things, we could not expect to locate such a Beauty. What any of us found 'attractive', whether in external goods or theories, would only be the product of Darwinian selection – and bear no relation even to what Darwin thought was true. It is not just our *moral* sense that would be wholly relative, but also our logical and epistemic sense. The fact that we (and other creatures) can be good engineers *demonstrates* that we have captured something real, and causally important. The beauty of things, and of the cosmos, identically is the form of being they shadow, copy, represent. If either logic, science or ethics is to avoid collapse we have to admit not just that Being Is, but also that It's beauty.

Suppose instead that Truth is ugly, boring, alien or frightful, and that there are other gods (or values) that demand our worship. That story might make sense if there was a world beyond 'the Truth', from which such alien values came to us. Even that Gnostic fantasy demands that the 'world beyond' has power in this. If we supposed instead that the gods we wish to serve are only, like ourselves, the products of a frightful truth, what possible allegiance could we feel to them? If God were worse than 'indifferent', what sense would there be in saying that our moral sense condemned Him? We cannot, in reason, argue against or vilify the Source of all our judgements.[31] Accordingly, we cannot hold that Truth is only one god amongst many, or that it is anything except the God of gods. If Truth is not what we can honestly esteem, there is nothing we can honestly esteem as more than a moment's pleasure.

So what is Beauty? What is it that excites in us such a 'delicious trouble', and binds us to acknowledge it? The beauty of a living face lies in its life, but even dead things may, on occasion, show themselves as beautiful: to be at all is to be beautiful, and our awakening to that beauty is also and equivalently an awakening to realize what Being is, at least in that small being. To become aware of beauty is, as Plato recognized, to be filled with beauty, a life that is, in itself, eternal. Being and Intellect and Beauty are the same. To be is

to be something, and all such somethings take their being from
the norms or forms contained in an eternal Intellect which shows
itself to us, in us, as beauty. When Weyl (and others) chose 'the
beautiful' above 'the true', he really meant to prefer the Truth
above what seemed, for the moment, to be true. It is a dangerous
step: we often realize, much later, that 'God has a higher
standard' of what's beautiful, that our initial judgement is
repaired when we come to see the real beauty of the real
solution.

Haldane, Lewis and Anscombe

Every time anyone points out the problem of a merely natur-
alized epistemology – that we have the beliefs, and axioms, and
methods that we do merely because they have been 'naturally
selected' – someone is sure to refer to 'Elizabeth Anscombe's
decisive refutation of C. S. Lewis's argument'. Anyone interested
in the history of that resilient mental microbe should read
Anscombe's own account, in the second volume of her collected
papers.[32] The first version of Lewis's argument was published in
the first edition of his *Miracles* (1947). Anscombe quite properly
criticized the formulation in her first published philosophical
work.[33] Lewis worked harder at the argument, and published a
much improved version in the second edition of *Miracles* (1960).
Anscombe recorded, in 1981, that she thought her criticisms of
the first version were just, as Lewis acknowledged, but that they
lacked 'any recognition of the depth of the problem'. She also
testified to Lewis's 'honesty and seriousness' in reconsidering the
argument, and to 'the depth and difficulty' of the issue. She
added that descriptions of the 1947 meeting as 'a horrible and
shocking experience which upset [Lewis] very much' did not fit
her own, or others', memory. I am told (by Anthony Kenny) that
Lewis himself did something to propagate the story, but no such
angst is visible in his rewritten version. Nor need it have been.

Lewis's argument was derived from Haldane. Haldane (himself a scourge of what he considered priestcraft)[34] argued as
follows:

If my opinions are the result of the chemical processes going
on in my brain, they are determined by the laws of chemistry,

not those of logic. If I believe that I am writing with real ink on real paper...I have no guarantee that this is true. I can only say that the chemical processes associated with that belief increase the probable duration of my brain, and various illusions may have this effect [including, successively, the chemical changes associated with belief, and disbelief in transubstantiation]....To put the matter in another way, if a super-biochemist made a working model of me, atom for atom, this robot would, on a Materialistic view, have all my memories. This may be the case, but if so no knowledge is possible.[35]

He added, in a footnote, that he did not find 'this argument' (which may be either the whole passage, or the concluding thought-experiment) as convincing as he did when he first wrote it.

The first reading of Haldane's argument suggests that opinions generated biochemically, and not 'by the laws of logic', can't be true. To this an obvious response is that clocks tell time by clockwork (and, nowadays, computers give right answers by turning switches on and off by rule). There is still a problem here: the clock does not 'tell time', nor does the computer calculate 'right answers', unless there is someone to interpret what is done. What 'beliefs' a chemical duplicate had would depend on the social and physical circumstances in which it was placed: they couldn't just be read off from the chemistry. Despite the efforts of materialists we still have no conception what material changes are equated with 'interpretation'. Clocks and computers are built so as to produce results that we can read as answers: but their being *answers* (right or wrong) is something different from any material state. There has to be some reference between the end-state of the computer and some features of the real, or humanly constructed world. 'Reference', again, is not a material state, like being six feet away, being square, or having a pH value of 5.3. Any of these features could be taken as referring – but that is still to rely on there being creatures to communicate, and recognize reality. So far from explaining how we can refer, or think, or feel, such merely material descriptions depend on our being able to.

Haldane's thought experiment was also meant to point out

the gap the story creates between our memories of doing something and our having done it: the replica 'remembers', but that gives it no clear warrant to believe that it performed the acts, or even that any did. Once we allow such biochemical control, we might create whatever deluded beings we wished: ones that 'remembered' being Sherlock Holmes or Moriarty. If that is actually our situation, how can we now trust our memories? To trust our memories, accordingly, is to assume that the biochemical story is not true, or at least not complete.

Again: if our opinions are determined by our biochemical conditions, and these in turn by 'the laws of chemistry', does it make sense to wonder if we *ought* to have those opinions? If my opinions are just chemical events, they may (let us suppose) be 'accurate' (at least under some interpretation), or even 'appropriate' (as aiding my survival), but they can't be something I *ought* or *ought not* to have. And in that case my beliefs aren't rational at all. Computers may have bugs, and clocks 'go wrong', but neither are irrational: their going 'wrong' is just as much an outcome of their earlier state as their going 'right'. Rationality insists that there are conclusions that we should not draw from certain premises: but 'drawing a conclusion' is only another chemical transformation which we can neither help nor hinder. Even the claim that p is true means that we *should* believe it. Chesterton raised a similar point about the status of 'good logic': 'Why should anything go right; even observation and deduction? Why should not good logic be as misleading as bad logic? They are both movements in the brain of a bewildered ape.'[36]

But the Haldane–Lewis argument (and Chesterton's) may have another point. Haldane's second sentence makes it clearer: not that a belief caused only by the motion of atoms can't be true (in some appropriate sense of 'true'), nor yet that there can be no *obligation* to accept it, but that there is no reason, if orthodox evolutionary theory is correct, to expect such beliefs to be true (whether that means 'accurate' or 'appropriate'). What matters is not whether they are caused, but how. Natural selection (as commonly described) only guarantees, at best, the inclusive genetic fitness of any inborn axioms or theoretical techniques, not their veracity or their value. Of course, they *might* be true: the flight of birds might presage the fall of kings (under some interpretation or another). It simply seems unlikely that it should unless the cosmos as a whole is 'in love with a real beauty'. This is in essence just the argument that Mackie used against the real existence of 'objective moral values': such values – he says – play no part in causing us to believe in them. We would still believe, he suggests, that infanticide was wrong even if there was no 'moral fact of the matter': accordingly, we have no reason to believe (he says) that, as a matter of fact, it is. I would agree with both Haldane and Mackie that whenever we know (or suspect) that the causes of our beliefs are radically detached from the supposed facts in which we believe, we would at least be wise to reconsider our beliefs – or rather, we would be if there were still any sense in wondering what is 'wise'. 'It is [hard], though of course possible, to worship one's own moral convictions, as Mr. Bertrand Russell does, while believing that they are an unimportant by-product of a universe which, as a whole, is indifferent to them.'[37] It is correspondingly hard, though of course possible, to worship one's own epistemological principles, while believing that they are an unimportant by-product of that self-same universe.

Is there an obvious retort, that those creatures who make bad guesses (about cliff-edges, predators and poisonous plants) die young? Must there not be a real advantage in getting things right, and therefore to such biochemical processes as make appropriate responses? But it is obvious – even if we take no notice of the evolutionary ages that preceded us – that almost all earthly creatures manage quite well without conceptions of discrete, continuing objects, or the truth, or reason. Mayr points out that eyes have evolved at least forty different times in different groups of animals:[38] human-style intelligence, as far as we can tell, evolved just once. It is also obvious (as Haldane points out) that it has often been advantageous to live by 'false' beliefs. He did not need to instance transubstantiation, or a disbelief in it, to make the point: each one of us 'believes' that her pains and pleasures, her family and friends, are more significant than those of other folk; each one of us 'believes' that future events are not as real as past ones; many of us 'believe' that God is 'on our side'. Maybe we are right to do so – but the beliefs in question are (it is quite plausible to say) embedded in us because they paid past generations, and not because they're true. Even what look to us like crass mistakes about local conditions aren't necessarily evolutionary dead-ends. And even if we could somehow be sure that creatures generally do 'get things right' about immediate conditions, why should we think that they would 'get things right' about the universe? Maybe bees convey accurate information about the whereabouts of flowers (because bee-hives whose bees did not, soon perished): why would that make it easier to understand why they should spend long winter nights conveying information about (say) stars, or the London Underground? The problem for us is that we insist (and must insist) that we can get things right (do get things right) about the universe in ways that can have had no possible advantage to our ancestors.

'Well, that's lucky. It just so happens that a complex of techniques originally selected for immediate advantage turns out to be the key to everything. Because our ancestors were good at getting meals, and avoiding being meals instead, and because our way of showing off (for mates) involved long speeches, gossip, and constructive fantasy, we have the power to imagine other worlds, and also to check those fantasies by seeing what local implications they would have. Somehow the power to count companions, or cattle, or sunrises, turns into a power to speak of elemental processes. How it works, who knows: it's enough that it does work.'

But that response depends on our assuming that it does: by exactly the same argument we can assert that, somehow, we are equipped to recognize 'objective moral facts'. Our belief that our successes show that we are right depends upon the judgement that we would be unlikely to be successful if we weren't. But, on our own account, uncounted species are successful without any notion of the World at Large, and the reason we have the theories that we do is because there was a practical advantage – or at least no relative disadvantage – to the relevant behaviour. The question remains: how likely could it be that chance-bred powers selected solely for their inclusive genetic fitness in the terrestrial environment would have the reach we think they do? Historically, we have believed in Reason because we believed that it was God who gave it. If we abandon that belief, our belief in Reason is as superstitious as belief in sacrifice. Why should our ways of counting be appropriate to a wider world, unless that world is really founded on principles that we discover in ourselves (as Galileo said)? And if we do find them there, it cannot be just because they used to 'pay'. By trusting in our intellect, we admit that Intellect is King, and that we are alert to the very same thing that works to make the universe one thing. On the other hand, if '[we] must realize that, like a gypsy, [we] live on the boundary of an alien world; a world that is deaf to [our] music and as indifferent to [our] hopes as it is to [our] sufferings or [our] crimes',[39] then it is ridiculous to expect our intellectual fancies to be any more at home.

SEVEN

DECENCY AND MORAL TRUTH

The Way of Knowledge

HINDU THOUGHT OFFERS a distinction between the ways of knowledge, action and devotion. Devotion to the deity, or to our own best image of the deity, may be the heart of 'true religion;'[1] right action, whether ritual or ethical, may be the face or outward form of it. The way of knowledge may seem dry or 'irreligious', and certainly has its own temptations and disasters. Not all those who speak of 'knowing the Mind of God' have any genuine belief that God is to be known, or worshipped. Their theism, even if sincere, may not be easily distinguished from atheism, and especially from an atheism that insists – however ineptly – on rational realism. Rational realists will often ask themselves what a genuinely rational agent *would* do: what is the simplest or the most elegant way of achieving the results, if all the power that could be wished were present? Guessing what such a one would do may sometimes help determine what in fact is done, even if the theorist does not quite believe that anyone or Anyone has done it. It may also help to see what anyone *should*, ideally, do. Is this presumption? Maybe the Stoics were right to think that the wise, but only the wise, have 'the Mind of God' (that Dion, if wise, was just as good as Zeus):[2] we may amuse ourselves by thinking what the wise, or God, would do, but why should we suppose that we, not being wise, would know?

Theism offers answers to the following problems: the mere existence of any thing that doesn't *need* to exist requires explanation; that any particular thing, and the cosmos, is a unity despite being spread about, requires an explanation; the existence of patterns in what does exist needs explanation; the existence of consciousness itself needs commentary; that we have any chance of discovering explanations itself requires explanation, and especially that this is so often by appeal to an intuited beauty. All I have sought to establish so far, after all, is that there is Something that exists, without coming into existence, by virtue of its nature, which is omnipresent (and so immaterial), that what is real is patterned in a way that requires the real existence of Mind (not the kind of mind we ordinarily have: fluctuating, self-deceived, impassioned, but the Mind on which we seek to model ours), that consciousness is not a weird addition to real being, and that the notion of knowledge itself requires a notion of Real Beauty. The pattern of things, or 'the Divine Intellect', needs nothing beyond itself, and has no plans. Such a doctrine is associated with Stoicism or with Spinoza – and all such philosophers have been regarded by orthodox believers as deceived. Even orthodox believers, of course, insist that we do not know everything, or even anything, about God's plans: it is dangerous to hypothesize what *must* be the case on the basis of what *we* think 'He should be doing'! His plans (if He has plans, if 'plans' are what He has) are not our plans. All times, places, entities and partial truths are alike to Him: nothing is lost, nothing is far away, nothing is any danger. 'Science', on this account, may indeed be our best route to God, since 'science' is founded in the wish to put aside humanity (though human scientists in fact, and understandably, forget this goal in all their ordinary occasions). Error lies in local allegiances, attachments, bodily sensations: truth lies in 'objectivity', 'impersonality', the abandonment of teleology or cultural affect. Philosophy, as Socrates said, is the practice of death.[3]

Maybe all that is true: maybe the spirit we need to incarnate the Divine Intellect is that 'scientific' spirit. By Aristotle's account the best and highest form of life is a form of contemplation which puts our ordinary humanity aside, and that life (he says) *is* God.[4] Certainly, he was right to insist that ordinarily ethical action could not be the life we should most choose to live. Really virtuous people do not want to find occasions to exercise their practical virtue: they don't wish others to be poor so they can exercise their liberality, nor wish for war so they can be courageous.[5] But I doubt if Aristotle, or other contemplative philosophers, would have agreed that what they contemplated didn't matter. Contemplation is a good thing (and it is good to encourage that spirit in ourselves) because the object of such contemplation is good and beautiful. A contemplation that dismantles what it contemplates, unweaves rainbows or clips angels' wings, is not the contemplative spirit that is intended. The real spirit of philosophical religion is not found amongst those who turn their fellow-creatures, or the cosmos, into *objects*. The truly scientific attitude, as Aristotle knew, is love: but 'love', in this context, is to wish that things exist, and prosper.

The real revolution in Copernican, and Galilean, theory was the claim to find out Truth: whereas earlier theorists only expected to discover useful fictions about Nature's underpinnings, the new breed of theorist believed that we could uncover the true story. In the last chapter I enquired how likely this could be, if we were indeed evolved, by Darwinian selection, from chance changes in the genes. There is no clear reason to believe that 'finding out the truth of things' could be more useful than inventing useful fictions: the opposite would seem more likely. In a merely Darwinian world there would be no reason to expect such powers, nor any reason to think them possible. If fantasists were to depict a species with a paranormal power of direct insight into subatomic structure, they would have to face two problems: what possible immediate advantage would such power give, and what possible mechanism could there be to accomplish it? In the absence of any answers, we would have to conclude that this was fantasy. But what is intellect itself if not that power? Either it is a fantasy (and we have no such insight into Truth) or there must be non-Darwinian reasons (as was argued in the previous chapter) for its being. If we have no insight into Truth, of course, we had better admit that we have no reason to believe (amongst other things) in neo-Darwinian theory, as a true account. Non-theistic answers to this puzzle rarely amount to more than mockery: mere demonstrations that the mocker hasn't understood the problem. We would only have good reason to expect such creatures as ourselves to know, or love, the Truth if something about the Truth requires, or makes it likely.

Consider 'scientific theism' for a moment longer. One way of developing it (one way that it has developed) is to suggest that things are as they are (the Truth is what it is) because nothing else is logically or mathematically possible. Explanation (whether of natural fact or of ethical demand) will end in logical truism. There will be no choice at all about what He thinks, since

He can only think what necessarily is true. That sort of theism will be indistinguishable, in practice, from atheism: such a God is bound by a necessity not of His making (and so He is not God). The conclusion for our conduct must in turn be that 'whatever is, is right': the Stoic sage has nothing to repent or to regret, since his enlightenment exactly is the recognition of necessity. It follows that we might reasonably hesitate to endorse a fully 'scientific theism': it certainly appears to be true that many features of the world are 'arbitrary', that many things that happen shouldn't, that 'some finite thing exists' is a thesis quite unlike most ordinary laws of logic. A more 'personalistic' theism seems to have the edge: by that account the final explanation will often be simply that Someone wanted things to be like that. Not everything is necessary, or right, and it is only true of God (the Infinite and Eternal) that it *must* exist (by necessity of its own nature). Isaac Newton spoke for many pious rationalists:

> Without all doubt this world could arise from nothing but the perfectly free will of God.... From this fountain ... [what] we call the laws of nature have flowed, in which there appear many traces indeed of wise contrivance, but not the least shadow of necessity. These therefore we must not seek from uncertain conjectures, but learn them from observations and experiments. He who is presumptuous enough to think that he can find the true principles of physics and the laws of natural things by the force alone of his own mind, and the internal light of reason, must either suppose that the world exists by necessity, and by the same necessity follows the laws proposed; or if the order of Nature was established by the will of God, that himself, a miserable reptile, can tell what was fittest to be done.[6]

Even rational realists, that is, can acknowledge that there are limits on what we can ourselves discover. If we could discover nothing, we could only live among our human fictions. If there is any hope of waking from that dream it must be, after all, that there is a point where we experience God. That point, the intellect, is not necessarily easy to uncover.

Pantheism: the Current Model

Stoic theory insists that there is only one possible universe: that universe is repeated, in an infinite succession, since everything so hangs together that any deviation is impossible. Modern theorists have been driven to conclude that there are after all contingencies: if everything were to fall back into the Big Crunch, and then begin again, it would not follow the same course as before – though we could obtain no evidence of other ages. It is a mark of desperation that some atheistical materialists have chosen to believe in infinite arrays of universes or of cosmic ages (amongst which, by chance, there is a world peculiarly well adapted to life and to intelligence) rather than believe instead that this well-adapted world is founded on intelligence. As I have observed before, if it were really true that anything that 'can' happen does, we would have to abandon rational enquiry. The idea of an infinitely long or infinitely large array of worlds, in which everything possible to happen sometimes or somewhere does, is a failed attempt at explanation – if everything possible happens sometime, it is less surprising that this (whatever it is) has happened. But it remains unclear why anything at all should happen: explaining away this world by saying that *all* worlds happen (which does not follow anyway merely from there being, we fantasize, an infinite array of worlds)[7] merely enlarges the problem – and destroys the basis of all explanation (since we could not, on those terms, be right to be surprised at *anything*, including Pratchett's Discworld). No finite thing, nor any array of finite things, can itself be necessary. No extended thing can itself be the source of unity. The only candidate for Necessary Omnipresence is immaterial.

But pantheism remains popular. Strangely, it has recently been suggested that we *ought* all to be pantheists, for the sake of a world which 'theists', it is said, have treated badly. The claim is a strange one: there is no actual evidence that 'theistic' cultures have done worse by the world than any others; there are clear directives within all branches of the Abrahamic tradition to respect the land, and the creatures that we share it with. On the other hand, for the last three centuries the Western imagination – which is blamed by the same critics – has been pantheistic. Western intellectuals, that is, have suggested that the material world is the inescapable context for all human action, and that there are no world-transcending duties. So far from its being the case that popular thought has urged us to be indifferent to material concerns, it has been taken for granted that matter is all that counts. If any single cultural explanation were sought for modern success in violating the environment it would be that insistence – though such simple explanations are more likely to mislead.

The questions are: what is pantheism, and why might it be thought the proper outcome for philosophical theology?

'Pantheism', in fact, may come in many colours.[8] The first – and the one that most concerns me here – is 'philosophical' or 'scientific' pantheism: the contention that the single Truth contains all truths by necessary derivation, and that there are no privileged points within that Truth. Everything that happens is an act of God, without distinction. The second, more 'romantic' pantheism emphasizes animistic sympathy or cosmic feeling: in moments like that we realize our unity with all that lives and is, and privilege those moments. The third sort of pantheism – and maybe the one that ecomystics actually endorse – is a way of saying that 'everything that lives is holy': the emphasis is not so much that the One God is everything, as that every individual thing is godly. It must already be clear that it is not easy to distinguish any of these forms from theism.

The One God that theists recognize is infinite: if there were a limit to the God, it would not be the necessary end of explanation. Because it is infinite every 'other' thing, however large or long-lived, is no more than finite: we may at first imagine that the All-Highest stands to us as we to ants, or to mitochondria (the energy-producing bodies present in eucaryotic cells). But to an Infinite Eye there is no difference in overt significance between ourselves and mitochondria and galaxies. The imagined god of eighteenth-century deists might plausibly be likened to a sultan, utterly indifferent to the welfare of the mice on board his ships. For an infinite deity an aeon and an afternoon, a garden and a galaxy, are equivalent: none absorb a larger share of energy or attention than any other. It seems to follow that nothing can be more significant to God than anything else. As the Wisdom of Solomon has it (11.24), God hates nothing that He has made: why else would He have made it?

Everything is as much a participant in Being as everything else; everything is as dependent on the Unity, on God's Attention, as everything else. Must this not conflict with traditionally hierarchical notions? 'Pantheism', on this account, differs from 'theism' in that human persons are no closer to the Infinite than bugs or quarks – and no more distant than the cosmic egg itself. Pantheism is an understandable response to an exaggerated anthropocentrism (though actual pantheists, paradoxically, were often more anthropocentric than monotheists were).

The physical cosmos, whether it is an aggregate or a real unit, is – on the present evidence – a finite one. The infinite God of theism, precisely because it is as close to every finite thing as to every other, and as easily attentive to it, is not to be identified with that cosmos. Maybe there is a single soul that animates this cosmos, but if there is it no more attends to us than we attend to mitochondria. As Plotinus saw, it is our sister, not our mother. Does this rule out the Christian axiom, that God was indeed incarnate as one particular creature? I shall argue shortly that some such incarnation is demanded. Would it return us to a pantheistic mode? A human person, after all, requires a cosmos to sustain it: of anyone it is literally true that the whole world is her body, since the light of the sun, and the respiration of algae, are essential to her bodily survival. If there is a human person who is God, then the whole world, centred on that person, is God's body. As further elements of that one body become obedient to God, the world is healed: we may, bizarrely, speak as if God's body is at present maimed by human or demonic rebellion. On this account, perhaps, God renews His involvement with the world of finite things by making them His body (as once, before His limbs rebelled, it was). Only because He is more than the cosmos can He heal the cosmos. Incarnation gives us all that honest pantheists can really want: at present we are not God, but hope to join Him.

Objective Values, Final Causes

The scientific revolution was itself an attempt at wakening, but one that has caused grave confusion. The thesis that there are no real 'objective values' rests on the rejection, for our scientific purposes, of final causes. That rejection, if it is more than a methodological convenience, leads to the death of reason. If there were no values, there would be no facts (since there would be nothing that we *should* believe). If values don't exist, then nothing does, and no one (since there could be neither defects nor responsibilities). Such nihilism has at least two forms: the radical, and the conventional. To reject them both is to adopt an older realism (once called Platonism). Of course there are truths that specify what we should do. Of course there are real standards to which things should aspire. Of course some things at least exist because they should. To understand why we have forgotten all this, we need to see why, for a while, we needed to forget.

The scientific revolution began with the denial of final causes. Instead of supposing that things existed 'to do good', or that we understand them best when we see what good they do, we chose instead to see simply how things happened: how, not why. Because we were no longer concerned (in scientific mode) with the good things did or might do we could no longer judge them more or less successful, more or less obedient. Instead of supposing that 'Nature does nothing in vain', let us instead suggest that everything that 'Nature does' is pointless. As Lucretius held, 'For nothing has been engendered in our body in order that we might be able to use it. It is the fact of its being engendered that creates its use.'[9]

This was a plausible response to an exaggerated anthropocentrism. Stoic pantheists, paradoxically, were less likely than Platonic theists to respect the real being of other creatures: for them, everything existed for the good of people. 'Bed-bugs are useful for waking us, and mice encourage us not to be untidy' (so Chrysippus said, according to Plutarch).[10] Pigs are no more than locomotive meals, with souls instead of salt to keep them fresh. Wetlands exist to be drained, and forests to be cut down. Were it not that exercise is good for us, the cosmos would have provided drainage ditches and cut planks to order. Not using the material for worthy ends is simply laziness, and what one tribe of people lazily ignore another may virtuously seize (as Engels said of California).[11] Spinoza's response seems apposite; 'in seeking to show that Nature does nothing in vain – that is, nothing that is not to man's advantage – they seem to have shown only this, that

Nature and the gods are as crazy as mankind.'[12] The fact that we can make use of things does not prove that they were made for us. And this is especially true if there are many things we cannot really use at all, or that run counter to any ordinary purposes of ours. As God said to Job:

> Who has let the wild ass of Syria range at will
> and given the wild ass of Arabia its freedom? –
> whose home I have made in the wilderness
> and its lair in the saltings;
>
> Does the wild ox consent to serve you,
> does it spend the night in your stall?
> (Job 39.5–6,9)

If we cannot tell what God intends (beyond the mere being of whatever things there are) we may as well not speculate. 'We shall entirely reject from our Philosophy the search for final causes; because we ought not to presume so much of ourselves as to think we are the confidants of His intentions.'[13] As Socrates concluded: even if everything is what it is, in essence, because it should be, we cannot trace that pattern, and had better concentrate on what there is, than why.

But that theistic reason for ignoring 'final causes' easily becomes a willed resistance to the very notion that there might be such. Because we plainly fantasized *some* purposes, it was assumed that all such purposes were fantasy. On this account there are no inbuilt norms. Without us, without our projected purposes, there could be no optical illusions, no zodiacal signs, no war-horses, no weeds. Less obviously, there are not even entities of the kind we usually think 'natural' (oaks, cattle, people). To be an oak-tree, after all, is to be something that grows according to a preset plan, against which deviation, accident or disease can be plotted. On the Stoic account even diseased oaks are as the cosmos truly requires them to be, but it is possible to identify them, locally, as trees that have not quite grown as they should, or as trees usually do. How do we identify a tree if there is no way, even locally, that they should grow? How do trees differ from convenient rock-formations? We can describe the latter, of course: that is, we can say that the rocky substance 'over there' reminds us of a pillar, or a bee-hive, or a human figure. But no one seriously thinks that those identifications are anything but subjective. That the rock looks like a bee-hive played no part in its growing where it did: it might as easily have looked like Aunt Agatha (perhaps it does). An acorn that is not even locally 'designed' to grow into an oak, and is much more likely to end up as supper, is not, objectively, an acorn, any more than it is, objectively, a present, a missile, a symbol or a philosophical example. Calling a piece of stuff, or an aggregate of elementary bits, by one name or another says nothing about what 'it' is. All we can truly say is that some elementary bits stay stuck together longer than some others.

Whereas Stoic moralists supposed that every creature aimed, or was aimed, at preserving its own being, Epicurean moralists identified pleasure (and the absence of pain) as what appetitive creatures (such as us) desired. Stoics reckoned that we felt pleasure ('normally') in activities we needed to perform to live. A fetishistic preference for pleasure even when it harmed us was, locally, irrational, even if the cosmos as a whole (apparently) required that some of us should make this 'error'. Epicureans, on the other hand, thought life could be worth living only if it brought us pleasure (principally, to avoid misunderstanding, pleasures of friendship, beauty, peace, that have no consequential pains attached). Whereas Stoic moralists reckoned that what things (really) were determined what use was to be made of them, an Epicurean moralist might think that any use was equally 'appropriate' (and therefore none was appropriate in the Stoic sense). Mice do not exist to keep us from being untidy, nor to encourage us (as they did Diogenes the Cynic) to travel light, nor even to produce more mice. They have no real purpose at all, and there is therefore no particular way to use them: they might as well be dinner, or art-objects, or grain-thieves. How many uses can you think of for a pebble, or for half-a-mouse?

Unregulated hedonism easily concludes, for example, that any pleasurable contact of two skins is 'as good' as any other. Whereas the older (post-Stoic) moralism reckoned that the proper use of sexual organs was made clear by 'Nature', more recent, radical 'amoralism' judges that anything can be the object and occasion of a 'sexual' desire. Sexuality, indeed, is nothing special. Masturbation, cunnilingus, fellatio, pederasty, bestiality, sodomy, necrophiliac practices, sado-masochism and fertile coition are all and only ways that some of us (does 'we' identify a real class?) get pleasure. None are more 'natural' than another, even if some are 'dangerous' or 'perverse' in the eyes of those who still believe that there are real entities involved. Any judgement between them can only be conventional, not natural. The same, presumably, applies in questions about diet: apples, grubs, mice, dogs and human babies are only conventionally distinguished. All are edible, and the different labels that 'we' make for them are only like the different labels that food-faddists give to different cuts of cow. 'No one who is anyone would serve rump-steak in place of tournedos, or long-pig in place of turkey for Thanksgiving Dinner.'

It would be wrong to assume that all 'Stoics' would defend the commonsense morality of Western Europe, or that all 'Epicureans' would despise it. On the contrary, it is a matter of record that those who believe in objective values, natural norms discoverable by reason, may decide – perhaps unwisely – that commonsense morality is wrong: incest, cannibalism and regicide may not be 'really' wrong precisely because there are some other things that are. One reason, oddly, why some moralists have denied that values could be objective is that they cannot let themselves believe that they themselves might be mistaken.[14] To avoid the possibility of any real challenge to their own moral convictions they prefer to found those convictions simply on their own determination to abide by them. The price of never being wrong, of course, is never being right. Conversely, those who disbelieve in objective values upon some other pretext may, for that very reason, adopt an unremarkable conventionalism: having no other standards to appeal to, and without any obligation to respect truth or consistency, they fall back upon contemporary custom. No one who is anyone takes stands. Some modern Epicureans even reinvent a kind of 'realism': if there are no real obligations, then the old distinction between facts that we were all bound to admit and fictions that could only bind a few (that is, between 'hard facts' and 'values') is inane. All truths (that is, all claims we should admit) are only conventionally binding, and therefore equally real. Stoics and others could distinguish 'truths by Nature' and 'truths by convention', what a man was 'really' worth and what he was worth 'in society'. All Epicureans can distinguish is what they value and what others do: why make a fuss?

But 'quasi-realists' are not my concern. The more interesting sort of radical objectivist has lost all faith in her own being. Being a person, or the same person as before, is being someone who can take responsibility for what one does, or who is held responsible. In the absence of real values, real responsibilities, there are no real persons, nor real identities. Whereas our realist predecessors could object to punishing a traitor's family for crimes that *he* did not commit, post-moderns have no warrant for the distinction. Such threatened 'punishments' would be deterrent, and we might as well insist upon the moral identity of a family or gene-line as of 'a single being'.

The visions which I have labelled 'Stoic' and 'Epicurean' have much the same effect. On Stoic terms the creatures with which we surround ourselves exist to serve our purposes. Cereals, cattle, horses, dogs and human slaves are judged good or bad according to their usefulness. All of them, in historical fact, have been bred and tamed so as to have some chance of being useful. Epicureans (reasonably) doubt the claim that any of these creatures came into existence for our sake. But for that very reason, that they exist for no one's sake, they can be used remorselessly for any purposes we have. Disenchanting Nature is only a device for making it available for purposes that were not countenanced (as being 'perverse') within the earlier, 'Stoic' synthesis. 'Objectifying a given domain involves depriving it of its normative force for us.'[15] 'From this point of view the conquest of Nature appears in a new light. We reduce things to mere Nature *in order that* we may conquer them.'[16] We do not *discover*, as so many think, that the world is normatively neutral: we reduce things to 'mere Nature' to be free of any normative demand. We invent the world of objects and then complain that such things can't show us how we should live (and so cannot even require us to acknowledge them as neutral).

What I have called 'Platonism' is a better route. The creatures who share the world with us exist (as the Stoics saw, in part) to embody and preserve real values. 'For in all natural things there is something wonderful.'[17] To be at all is to be *something*, and the thing in question is identified as worth knowing, and worth existing by the very effort with which whatever is persists in being. As Spinoza saw, following the Stoics, 'the effort with which each thing endeavours to persist in its own being is nothing but the essence of the thing itself'.[18] To understand it is to see why it exists, and to see that it can never be merely a means to some other creature's good.[19] It exists because God wants it to: its existing *is* its wanting to exist.

Platonists can 'analyse' as well as any. Even if their efforts do not wake us up, they may still help to persuade us that we are awake when we experience Otherness, and when we see things in the light of Day. In the insane person's universe everything is targetted at him or her. As Wittgenstein said: 'What has history to do with me? Mine is the first and only world! I want to report how I found the world!'[20] To this there can, in a way, be no reply except to hope that 'the hammer of a higher God could smash [this] small cosmos, scattering the stars like spangles, and leave [him] in the open, free like other men to look up as well as down'.[21] But demoralizing Nature may be a necessary discipline. When Wittgenstein urges us to 'remember that the spirit of the snake, of the lion, is [*our*] spirit'.[22] He can only seriously be speaking of the spirits of moralized snakes or lions, heraldic beasts. In order to avoid interpreting snake or lion behaviour in that inappropriate way, and to recall the projected spirits, we may reasonably insist, for a while, that we will only speak of their 'objective movements', motions that have no moral weight (beyond the mere, remaining implication that we should face the facts).

If, for a while, we have allowed ourselves to think 'objectively' (and so to incur these problems) it was only to purge Nature (Nature, that is, as we experience it) of our own conceits. Just so, Chesterton suggested, Christians of the early middle ages had to turn aside from Nature for a while. Gardens, woods and the stars themselves were polluted (that is, the world of Nature as it features in our imaginative experience was polluted) by the perversions of late paganism.[23] Only when four centuries of ascetic practice had purified the imagination could St. Francis rededicate the natural world. 'Man has stripped from his soul the last rag of nature-worship, and can return to nature.'[24] When we can face the world as Other than ourselves, we can at last interpret it. Neither objectivists nor quasi-realists do either. Stoics and Epicureans did make the attempt, but lost their way. It is precisely because things-in-themselves are worth knowing, because they embody real values, that we ought to rise above immediate prejudice, personal affections and dislikes, projected spirits. If there were no real values independent of our will there could be no real reason to transcend our prejudice.

A Personal God

But how *personal* can God be? Does God have plans for us? That question is, deliberately, crude. The God of the Philosophers (and, as I suppose, of Abraham) needs nothing from us or from any creature; He needs no help from 'secondary causes' to create whatever state of the world He wishes. What He creates He wishes: whatever is sustained in being, therefore, is not to be valued only instrumentally. It exists 'because God chooses that it should', because it is the partial expression of the life and Intellect of God. Seeing 'as God sees' (or with as close an approximation as is possible for human eyes) is to see the good in everything, to see how there is something that *should* be, whatever faults or accidents we cannot help identifying as what *shouldn't* be. As we noted earlier, He hates nothing that He has made: why then would He have created it? That balance between endorsement and rejection is the subject of religious and ethical dispute and practice, and a larger topic than I can embark on here. One metaphysical distinction worth highlighting is between *substance* and *event*: whereas some post-moderns have insisted that this distinction is an artefact, an inference from Indo-European grammar, it is in fact an ethical axiom. Without such a distinction it would be impossible to hate the sin and love the sinner, since 'sinners' would be aggregated sins.

In brief: we can encourage in ourselves, and pray for, a truth-speaking spirit, by whose influence we see the world in the light of the Divine Intellect that is awakened in us. In seeing things like that we understand that there is something 'even beyond being', a reason why anything at all that might not exist actually does: the Good (or the One). Part of that One's product is as necessary as Itself: there is no way that It could generate another standard than the one embodied in the Intellect.[25] It is significant that Christian orthodoxy and Muslim orthodoxy alike have concluded that the very Word of God is, strictly, uncreated.[26] Part of what exists (according to the orthodox) is strictly 'arbitrary'. It is something 'chosen', as it were, out of immensity. But we can be sure that whatever is the case will rest on beauty, and be capable of further beauty, further involvement in the divine. We cannot thence deduce exactly what the case may be. The world is partly contingent, partly as it must be. Correspondingly, if it is possible for us (being human) to embody the divine, it must at least be *possible* for someone to be both human and divine, without diminution or mixture. Those acquainted with traditional (Christian) theism must by now have recognized that I am playing with the Creeds: God is simultaneously Father, Son and Spirit; and the Son is incarnate, being both human and divine. We share that life, in our degree, by the inspiration of the spirit, and thence conclude that we will share in it forever. Other branches of the Abrahamic tradition may dispute the details of the incarnation: traditionally, they too acknowledge that there is at once a difference and identity between the One (the Father, God) and God's true Word (whether that is Jesus, or the Torah, or the Koran). For my present, compendious purposes, the real differences between traditions matter less than the identities.

Theism depends on two assertions: first, that everything (and every thing) depends on God for its continued being; second, that God Himself is still distinct from all dependent beings. If He were sheerly distinct (distinct as finite beings are distinct) He would after all be only one thing among many, having no strong claim to be more than (at most) the eldest, biggest, strongest. It is not impossible that there is some one such being, somewhere. It is not impossible that different beings are differently superior, or that there is no being which is clearly top in any range of excellence. None of that has anything to do with God. 'God' does not name a being who has a high, or even the highest, score upon a range of excellences: 'God' names the standard of such excellence, and hence is unsurpassable. On the other hand, if every thing were only a dependent piece of God (as Stoics and Spinoza sometimes speak) then theism would be indistinguishable from dangerous forms of pantheism (which is the end of reason: all thoughts and actions would be God's alone, and faultless). African theologians have seen the point as well as European: when the Nuer say that rain, lightning or pestilence *is*

God (*e kwoth*), they nonetheless deny that God *is* rain, lightning or pestilence.[27] Any Creator God does, in a way, become one being amongst many: that self-limiting implies that creation is always incarnational. But that incarnate deity is also the One beyond.

There is no logical difficulty here, though there are tensions. Everything exists by courtesy of Being, and every thing is an image of some perfection in the Divine Intellect. On the other hand, those images are now imperfect, fallen. Each thing, in the moment of its being, tends to want to win, to seize things for itself, to be the only image. The world of individuals we now inhabit is, as Plotinus quite as much as Paul believed, a fallen world. There is an unfallen world, the Intellect: one question is whether anything discovered Here enhances what is There? What value could there be in fallen worlds, that does not exist in the Unfallen? And how, if there were such, could it be retrieved?

This issue, of evil and atonement, raises problems larger than philosophers can handle. Berkeley had cause to mock: 'he who undertakes to measure without knowing either [the measure or the thing to be measured] can be no more exact than he is modest,... who having neither an abstract idea of moral fitness nor an adequate idea of the divine economy shall yet pretend to measure the one by the other.'[28] But there is nonetheless an answer. We do not know how many dangers God has chosen to realize: it may well be that most of them remain fictitious, unrealized by any soul. The ones that He has chosen (namely ours) are ones that, we suppose, He has sought to solve. How to go on being virtuous in times of drought and fear: what is the shape that virtue makes amongst the heathen? Maybe that is a sufficient answer: what we know, God knows; what we endure, we live through by His grace. But we may still be disturbed to think that Being imposes costs upon His creatures that He cannot bear Himself. Even if God experiences what we do, even with utmost empathy – this is only to say that there is a God's eye view of suffering such that, managing to take it, we feel less disturbed. But in that case God Himself, the Omnipotent, can't really suffer, and changes what we experience in knowing it. The way that we remember suffering might give a clue: remembered pain is rarely itself painful (remembered embarrassments are an exception!). Even present pains, so long as they are not extreme, can be evacuated of their painfulness by mental discipline. Maybe that is how a god would see them: as facts that carried no affective force at all. Such a god, though formally omniscient, would never understand us. The only option that looks plausible must be that somewhere, and some time, the Omnipotent must Himself become an ignorant individual, and suffer as we do, so that He can manage real sympathy and support for us: without this there are things He does not know.

That God should be incarnate is a postulate of reason: without such incarnation we would doubt His virtue, and also doubt that He could really know or understand our case. Doubting God's virtue is of course insane: to do so must cast doubt on everything we do or think. If the source of all our judgements can't be trusted, what value do those judgements have? 'What beauty can be found in a moral system, formed, and governed by chance, fate or any other blind, unthinking principle [or still less a malevolent or foolish one]?'[29] Why should we suppose that the impulses accidentally bred into us form any sort of coherent, admirable or long-lasting whole? That, after all, is the reason why we need, being rational realists, to be theists. To avoid insanity we must believe that God is, somewhere, what we are, or should be. It does not follow that the Christian story is exactly true: maybe what is said of Jesus should be said of someone else instead. In that sense Christianity does not entirely depend on history: even if that story turned out false, we could be Christians, dependent on the promise that a story of that sort would someday be true (or rather, *is* true at some time and place).

That incarnation is a truth of reason may answer other questions: what is it that God does in making real things, which aren't confined by God's own Intellect? In effect, God makes Himself one being among many: in one sense He remains as Being, the root of every existent thing; in another there are, by grace, as many other beings as He wills. To be one among many is, in effect, to be incarnate: to be distinguishable as God from many things that, in a way, aren't God. The question would be: where is that locus of God's identity, the one being who is also

Being? Once again, there is no philosophical certainty that the answer is Jesus, son of Mary: it is enough that it really might be.

Reason and Revelations

It must be firmly fixed in our memory as the supreme infallible rule that those things which have been revealed to us by God must be believed to be the most certain of all. And that although perhaps some spark of the light of reason might seem to very clearly and evidently suggest to us something else; nonetheless, trust must be placed solely in divine authority rather than in our own judgement.[30]

Perhaps the human heart and mind is so corrupt as to have lost, or never to have had, a grip on Truth (or what stands in for Truth). Perhaps, as I have said before, such creatures as we are revealed to be by scientific reason never could expect to get a grip on Truth: why should we suppose that creatures evolved with the kind of 'intelligence' they need to get their next meal, or avoid being one, could somehow acquire the knack of discovering their own past history, or the universe's? Revelation is, perhaps, all that we can hope for.

To those anti-rationalists who prefer to keep faith solely with the revealed Word, Augustine has a charitable reply:

Those who exult in divine assistance and who glory in being able to understand and to treat the sacred books without precepts of the kind which I have undertaken to supply herewith, so that they think these precepts superfluous, should calm themselves for this reason: although they may rightfully rejoice in the great gift God has given them, they should remember that they have learned at least the alphabet from men.[31]

Even those who rely on revelation must also rest on reason and tradition, and need to think through the arguments which identify the possibility of Truth and its discovery. 'It by no means becomes a philosopher to accept as true something which he has never perceived to be true; and to trust in his senses, that is, the unconsidered judgements of his childhood, more than in mature reason.'[32] On the other hand, it was the supposed father of modern rationalism, Descartes, who suggested that God *made* the laws of logic, and impressed an image of His truth upon our hearts and minds that yet was not identical with that same Truth. 'They are all inborn in our minds just as a king would imprint his laws on the hearts of all his subjects if he had the power to do so', and are such that 'He could change them as a king changes his laws.'[33] If even the laws of logic are impressed in us, why may not God have impressed other laws? And why may He not have done so in our infancy? Is the difference only between those laws that have been universally (have they?) impressed and those which are more local? But if God 'makes up logic' we cannot be so sure that He has not made up a different logic for His other tribes.

Others thought, perhaps with justice, that Descartes' judgement was heretical – amounting indeed to the claim that God has 'made' the Word, and also that it is not the Word Himself in us, but only a feeble copy. On both counts, Descartes here strayed from orthodox theism, and sound sense. But though we may be sure that God Himself is 'logical' (and holy) we cannot always tell what logic should demand. Reality is not limited by what we here can conceive, and although we should be guided by the laws of logic we should not believe that we are the best judges of what strictly is illogical. We have too often been misled. Surely only one line can be drawn perpendicular to the line ——— from any given point along it? But now, in your mind's eye, move that line an inch forward from the paper – and lo, an infinite number of such lines are possible.[34] Surely nothing can fall from a finite distance toward the earth, and not be diverted, and yet not reach the earth? But remember that the earth's surface falls away as well: an object in free fall, from a sufficient distance, simply orbits round. Can anything be red and green all over at the very same time, or anything be both in motion and at rest? Yes. No doubt whatever is the case must in the end be other than what isn't: to affirm anything to be the case is to deny its opposite – but we are often less acute than we suppose in seeing what real opposites, in some particular circumstance, may be. From which it follows that we may suspect some revelations, if they seem 'illogical', may just be riddles. And what we think is certain may legitimately be disbelieved by those with clearer access to the

One True Reason. To think anything else than that is just conceit – but we should still attempt to solve the riddles.

Ought we to obey God whatever we may think of what He orders? Could He rightly require us to do what hitherto we've thought was wrong, and would it then be right? Those who raise the question usually reveal that they have mistaken what 'God' means. We can certainly ask, of any finite being's word, whether it is true: we cannot sensibly enquire if God is true. God *is* the Truth, conceived (as I have argued) as the infinite, immaterial, necessity of Being. To say of anything that it is real, is to say that God sustains it; to say of anything that it is true, is to say that God maintains it. Nor is the case any different in matters of obligation: to say that this is what we *ought* to do is to say that it is God who requires it. To ask whether we *ought* to do what God requires is pointless. We might as well enquire whether we ought to do what is our obligation – and indeed some few philosophers have realized that any difficulty there is in affirming our duty to obey God's Word will also be a difficulty about affirming any duty. If there is a fact of the matter about what we should do, might it not make sense to ask why we should pay attention to that fact? Some have concluded that there can be no such fact: moral realism, they say, conflicts with true morality. No one should ever do anything on the plea that, whatever they or anyone else may think, it's really right. To which the only sensible reply must be: who says? Those who claim 'the moral high ground' in saying that we *ought* not to do things just because we ought, are living in confusion.

So if God commanded sacrifice, we should? Of course: but that is no more surprising than to say that if it were right to sacrifice, we should. What makes an act obligatory if not that it is demanded by That Than Which None Greater Can Be Conceived? If there are no such obligations, we cannot in reason be obliged to anything. And in that case, we have no obligation even to talk sense. The necessary postulate of reason is that there are errors: things we should believe and don't, or shouldn't believe and do. But that is just to say that Truth is God, that the felt demand to serve It just is what we mean by 'moral obligation'.

Moral reason rests in the conviction that we may have real duties, and that, in the end, there are no moral inconsistencies, no cases where one ought to do what another ought to prevent. That claim, however necessary for our moral reason, is not always easy: maybe our fallen nature just is this – that sometimes we ought not to do the very things we ought – and will be guilty of something whatever it is we do. Some schools conclude that moral reasoning is relative, that there are no truthful answers. Others that we ought to pay the price. If there are no truthful answers, then (again) there are no duties to talk sense, consult the evidence or follow truth.

Kant's argument (which was also Plotinus's) concludes that we are free because we know that we have duties: if we were not, it couldn't make sense (despite the efforts of Stoicizing sages) to think that we *should* do anything except what actually we do (and were always going to do). The Stoic sage regrets nothing, not even the 'errors' of others, or his own. Our freedom does not rest upon our being subject to no obligations but our own, but in our being obliged to Intellect, which is the Word of God. It is because there is that Intellect, the very same in every finite thing, that it is sensible to test our moral intuitions by enquiring whether *everyone* could be supposed to be ordered to do the same. If they couldn't be, then that cannot be what the Intellect requires. It doesn't follow that God cannot issue individual instructions, but only that the ones He issues will also be compatible with general duty. Without such theism, Kantian morality does not make sense: consequently, Kant cannot be invoked against 'Divine Command Morality'. Those who imagine otherwise have forgotten what he meant.[35]

And what is the divine command? To hate nothing that He has made.

EIGHT

COMMUNITIES OF FAITH

The Importance of Tradition

ALTHOUGH I HAVE sought to identify reasons for accepting philosophical, and biblical, theism which are accessible to any rational intelligence, I make no claim that all and only those theses that such an abstract intelligence would invent or accept are properly acceptable. As George Berkeley insisted, if we really attempted to put aside all 'prejudice', all opinions taken upon trust, we should find ourselves entirely destitute. 'If we were left, every one to his own experience, [we] could know little either of the earth itself or of those things the Almighty has placed thereon: so swift is our progress from the womb to the grave.'[1]

On the other hand, we are all infected by opinions and assumptions we could do without. Without occasional spring-cleaning our minds grow stale: the question is, what *can* we do without? Descartes presented his philosophy as a new – or at least his own – way of securing old truths, but there are points on which Cartesian thought does differ from other versions of 'the perennial philosophy'. On the one hand, the effect (though not, I suspect, the intention) of Descartes' argument was to push the evidence of testimony – and experience in general – aside: all that we could be sure we knew was what we could see clearly and distinctly to follow from the central axioms. God would not deceive us if we sought to see exactly what presents itself, but the whole drift of Enlightenment epistemology is to deny us any right to rest content with what we're told about the past. This is odd: if I can trust my own senses, why may I not trust yours, or anyone's? And if I can't trust what you say, why may I trust my notes? Berkeley, of course, did recognize that there was no substitute for testimony: 'so swift is our passage from the womb to the grave' that no one could learn much by her own experience.[2] Augustine too had accepted the conclusion:

In order to contemplate eternal truth in a way that will enable us to enjoy it and cling to it, a path through temporal things, suited to our infirmity, has been marked out for us, namely, that we accept on faith past and future events so far as this suffices for men on their journey towards things eternal. These teachings of faith are so regulated by God's mercy as to give them the greatest authority.... We must readily believe them because they help us very much to strengthen our hope and to arouse our love.[3]

Although Descartes repeatedly insisted that we could not know what seemingly possible world God had actually created, and could not therefore reach the truth by reasonings alone,[4] his actual cosmological practice was far more dogmatic, and his physical theories as distant from any real truth as the concluding myth of Plato's *Phaedo*. This is indeed the chief fault that modern philosophers have found with him: that he supposed that knowledge could be created by one lonely intellect, distrustful of everything that others seemed to say. Strangely, it is now common doctrine that we must begin from commonsensical, shared knowledge, although free-thinkers denigrate the testimony of any other group than theirs. Strangely, commentators continue to extol the virtues of 'mere empiricism', although it is clear that all our experience is mediated by inherited structures which might, we can conceive, be otherwise. Where Augustine (and Berkeley) reckoned it good evidence for the truth of teachings that they 'help us very much to strengthen our hope and to arouse our love', our sages prefer those teachings which confirm us in that muddle of 'objectivity' and anthropocentric pride that passes for common sense today.[5]

Testimony and the Inner Light

George Berkeley philosophized at the beginning of the Cartesian Era, so to call it: that period when philosophers were expected to divest themselves of prejudice, even if only to place their commonsense beliefs on a more secure foundation. 'Our affections should grow from inquiry and deliberation else there is danger of our being superstitious or Enthusiasts.... It is our duty to strive to divest our selves of all byas whatsoever.'[6]

In our nonage while our minds are empty and unoccupied many notions easily find admittance, and as they grow with us and become familiar to our understandings we continue a fondness for them. ... But we would do well to consider that other men have imbibed early notions, that they as well as we have a country, friends, and persons whom they esteem. These are pleas which may be made for any opinion, and are consequently good pleas for none.[7]

To strip the soul of prejudice is an ancient nostrum. Witness Edward Herbert, British Rationalist: 'those who would enter the shrine of truth must leave their trinkets, in other words their opinions, at the entrance, or as one might say in the cloakroom. They will find that everything is open or revealed to perception as long as they do not approach it with prejudice.'[8] This is a commonplace (also to be found in John Colet and in Luther,[9] derived from Philo's allegory whereby (as in an earlier chapter) the High Priest must strip off the soul's tunic of opinion and imagery to enter the Holy of Holies,[10] and from Plato's story of Glaucus.[11] It is very difficult to strip, 'since the veils of prejudice and error are slowly and singly taken off one by one'.[12] It is, on the other hand, very easy to *think* that one has done it, and that our own, conscientiously 'modern' opinions are so obviously founded on right reason that we do not need to argue for them. In his *Guardian Essays* Berkeley refers to gentlemen (likewise 'freethinkers') who 'did not think themselves obliged to prove all they said, or else proved their assertions, by saying or swearing they were all fools that believed the contrary'.[13] It is one thing to recognize that we may have imbibed errors: quite another to discover some rule by which we may identify them.

That rule clearly cannot simply be to 'weed out of [our] minds and extirpate all such notions or prejudices as were planted in them before they arrived at the free and entire use of reason.'[14] There may be many things that we cannot ourselves prove which are still true, and which we have good reason to accept as true. If we really attempted to put aside all 'prejudice', all opinions taken upon trust, we should find ourselves entirely destitute. Even if a few brilliant intelligences could cope with believing all and only what they themselves have 'proved', that cannot be the normal condition of humanity (as, incidentally, Descartes knew quite well).

It follows that those of us who do attempt to follow Philo's rule must still accept some propositions without proof, and those (the majority) who don't had better hope that they have all been well enough brought up:

> There must... of necessity, in every State, be a certain system of salutary notions, a prevailing set of opinions, acquired either by private reason and reflection or taught and instilled by the general reason of the public, that is, by the law of the land.... Nor will it be any objection to say that these are prejudices; inasmuch as they are therefore neither less useful nor less true, although their proofs may not be understood by all men.... The mind of a young creature cannot remain empty; if you do not put into it that which is good, it will be sure to receive that which is bad. Do what you can, there will still be a bias from education; and if so, is it not better this bias should lie towards things laudable and useful to society?... If you strip men of these their notions, or, if you will, prejudices, with regard to modesty, decency, justice, charity, and the like, you will soon find them so many monsters, utterly unfit for human society.[15]

Does it follow, as Boswell archly enquired of Johnson, that 'a poor Turk must be a Mahometan, just as a poor Englishman must be a Christian'?[16] No Abrahamist can be altogether happy with that conclusion, granted that we might be called to abandon all our household gods. But we cannot simply ignore them. Nor can we rely only on a version of the Cartesian rule: to believe only those propositions which it is impossible ('logically impossible') to deny. It is true, no doubt, that I cannot coherently deny that I exist, nor that there is a truth which transcends my thought of it. It may even be true, as I have been arguing, that this Truth must be God – the infinite free Spirit. But 'nothing could be more vain and imaginary than to suppose... that the whole world... might be produced by a necessary consequence of the laws of motion' [or the original structure of the world].[17] We may wish to insist that the Truth does, after all, contain all truths, and that God, in knowing them, makes them definite, but they remain, for us, beyond all argument. It does not follow that we cannot, with patience, 'know' them, but not with 'scientific or demonstrative knowledge'. Even God cannot know them save by observation (on which see earlier remarks about the Divine Soul) and enactment.

We cannot expect to demonstrate the truth of everything worth believing. We cannot even suppose that we should only believe what has always been believed by everyone: 'diversity of opinions about a thing doth not hinder but that thing may be, and one of the opinions concerning it may be true.'[18] Nor can we evade our own responsibility for what we choose to accept as true. Berkeley's letter to his friend John James, on the occasion of James' conversion to the Church of Rome argues that even if it were true that there is an objectively infallible guide, we could not locate such a guide without a prior trust in our own capacity to do so. 'Of what use is an infallible guide without an infallible sign to know him by?'[19] 'We see ... with our own eyes, by a common light but each with his own private eyes. And so must you or you will not see at all. And not seeing at all how can you chuse a Church? Why prefer that of Rome to that of England? Thus far, and in this sense every man's judgment is private as well as ours.'[20]

On the one hand, it must be I that judge what to believe; on the other hand, this I, and the principles on which it acts, are as debateable as any. 'We would do well to consider that other men have imbibed early notions, that they as well as we have a country, friends, and persons whom they esteem' ... and an identity.

So must I conclude that my conclusions are not to be relied upon? They may not be, but I can no more conclude to this, in practice, than to a denial that I exist or think. 'At any street corner we may meet a man who utters the frantic and blas- phemous statement that he may be wrong. Of course his view must be the right one, or it is not his view!'[21] Being corrected is a death – and resurrection. I must suppose that there is that in me – the intellect – which can be trusted, and must also reject all theories which deny that fundamental faith. 'True it is that prejudices early imbibed and sunk deep in the mind are not immediately got rid of; but it is as true that in every Humane Creature there is a ray of common sense, an original light of reason and nature which the worst and most bigoted education, although it may impair, can never quite extinguish.'[22] 'There is an indwelling of Christ and the Holy Spirit, there is an inward light. If there be an *ignis fatuus* that misleads wild and conceited men, no man can thence infer there is no light of the sun.'[23] 'Intellect and reason are alone the sure guides to truth'[24] – which is, emphatically, not to say that secular reason is.

'I, among a number of persons who have debauched their natural taste, see things in a peculiar light, which I have arrived at, not by any uncommon force of genius or acquired knowledge, but only by unlearning the false notions instilled by custom and education.'[25] This youthful boast relies upon the notion of 'natural taste', true light – a reliance Berkeley did not surrender. In Augustine's words:

> Turn where you will, wisdom speaks to you by the imprint it has left on its works, and when you are slipping back into what is outward, it entices you to return within by the beauty of those very forms found in things external.... You must come to see that it is not possible to pass judgment, favorable or unfavorable, on things known by the bodily senses unless you have at your disposal a knowledge of certain laws governing beauty to which you refer whatever objects you perceive outwardly.[26]

But in trusting that original light we must, as Berkeley made clear, accept that it is not just our own. 'Our present impending danger is from the setting up of private judgement, or an inward light, *in opposition to human and divine laws*.'[27] Those who 'flatter themselves that they alone are the elect and predestinate of God, though in their lives and actions they show a very small degree either of piety toward God or charity toward man'[28] are no good models. If there is a light in me, it must also be in others, and in the original judgement of humanity, however far defiled or damaged. There are false and dangerous opinions loose in the world, and many failures of intelligence, but if we are not to despair entirely of ever speaking truth, we must believe that there is a truth within tradition, and that, by faithful obedience to the light, we can uncover more. Unlearning *everything* on the plea that it might be false is both impossible and self-defeating. As

Herbert said: 'Reason is the process of applying common notions as far as it can, and has nothing beyond them to which it can appeal. Common Notions, therefore, are principles which it is not legitimate to dispute.'[29] 'Anyone who prefers persistently and stubbornly to reject these principles might as well stop his ears, shut his eyes and strip himself of all humanity.'[30] In Berkeley's words: 'We who believe a God are entrenched within tradition, custom, authority and law': why abandon that advantage at the will of a free-thinker?[31]

> The more we think, the more difficult shall we find it to conceive how mere man, grown up in the vulgar habits of life, and weighed down by sensuality, should ever be able to arrive at science without some tradition or teaching, which might either sow the seeds of knowledge, or call forth and excite those latent seeds that were originally sown in the soul.[32]

In sum: self-styled free-thinkers who spoke out against 'religious prejudice' necessarily relied on prejudice themselves, while simultaneously denying themselves the right to do so.[33] Those who say there is no inner light at all, cannot coherently trust their own judgement; those who say that testimony and inherited opinion must all be abandoned condemn themselves to an incorrigible ignorance. Those who claim the inner light entirely for themselves (as though the Truth should enlighten them and no one else) are the first victims of 'an inward conceited principle... sufficient to dissolve any human fabric of polity or civil government.'[34] If we should believe what cannot (coherently) be denied, we should believe in the possibility of finding truth 'by consulting [our] own minds, and looking into [our] own thoughts'[35] – always recalling that many of those thoughts were conveyed to us by others.

The Limits of Understanding

But what sort of truths, if any, do religious utterances – apart from theological theorems of the kind I have been discussing – convey? We cannot dismiss them, as free-thinkers do, merely because we cannot 'prove' them (cannot show that they follow, by free-thinkers' rules, from axioms accepted by free-thinkers).[36]

The rules and axioms of free-thinkers are also taken upon trust, and are less acceptable than religious rules and axioms just because they claim that nothing should be taken upon trust. But perhaps religious utterances (or those of some traditions) are so obscure, or so absurd, that we should, after all, abandon them. We may sensibly believe what can't be proved: can we sensibly believe what can't be understood? It must seem clear that we can't.

Berkeley's response, as so often, is *ad hominem*: 'that philosopher is not free from bias and prejudice who shall maintain the doctrine of force and reject that of grace, who shall admit the abstract idea of a triangle, and at the same time ridicule the Holy Trinity.'[37] And again: 'with what appearance of reason shall any man presume to say that mysteries may not be objects of faith, at the same time that he himself admits such obscure mysteries to be the objects of science?'[38]

> To me it seems evident that if none but those who had nicely examined, and could themselves explain, the principle of individuation in man, or untie the knots and answer the objections which may be raised even about human personal identity, would require of us to explain the divine mysteries, we should not often be called upon for a clear and distinct idea of a person in relation to the Trinity, nor would the difficulties on that head be often objected to our faith.[39]

At least two answers are possible. First, we might agree that there is much that we do not understand, in science and common sense, and yet deny that we should therefore pretend to accept yet more uncomprehended dicta. Second, we might insist that the oddities of current physical theory, the contradictions of mathematical practice, or the difficulty of giving an acceptable analysis of current common sense, are all temporary failings. We cannot imagine eleven-dimensional space–time; we may not (yet) be able to do without such contradictions as Berkeley identified in Newton's calculus; we may not have a good account of personal identity for the same reason that we have no good account of bogeys. Some day (perhaps) we shall discover 'God's true language' or 'the Mind of God': the fact that our present language has its flaws is no good reason to retreat to a still earlier, worse one. 'Science' (as a general title) is progressive:

'religion' is conservative. Failings in science will be corrected; those of religion are inescapable.

My experience suggests quite otherwise. Those who think of themselves as 'scientists', and especially those who most despise the dogmas of religion, are often wilfully dogmatic. Any attempt, for example, to challenge the right of scientists to experiment invasively on animals is met with scorn (though there have been some improvements). Any suggestion that a scientific degree, or a career in 'science', does not necessarily make one an authority on historical, or theological, or moral matters, is rebuffed. This is unsurprising: clerisies, of their nature, tend toward conceit. Theologians, in the present day, are far more sensitive to criticism: sometimes, excessively. The individual failings of particular scientists, or theologians, of course, do not necessarily do great damage to the institutions. Vice can be made to serve the ends of virtue – but the service is made harder by conceit.

Berkeley might respond in turn that the issue is not about what we should *add* to our belief-system, but about what we have reason to reject. The argument is not that because physicists believe in wave–particle duality they might equally believe, on the authority of Lewis Carroll's *Jabberwocky*, that borogoves are mimsy. Berkeley is himself responding to an attack: if it is difficult to analyse the doctrine of the Trinity, or be sure exactly what its implications are, this is itself no reason to reject the doctrine. For if it were, we should have exactly the same reason to reject much physical and mathematical theory, as well as common sense. 'I do not therefore conclude a thing to be absolutely invisible, because it is so to me.... [and] dare not pronounce a thing to be nonsense because I do not understand it.'[40] Berkeley's prejudice is to keep as close to common sense[41] as possible, even if that sense should also be purged of outright error and infidelity. We are entitled (as above) to go on believing things we cannot prove, and ones whose implications we do not altogether understand. We are entitled to prove sophisms false by doing the things that sophists say we can't.[42] Belief, of course, is not displayed in verbal repetition, and certainly not the repetition of abstract formulae:

> There is ... a practical faith, or assent, which sheweth itself in the will and actions of a man, although his understanding

may not be furnished with those abstract, precise, distinct ideas, which, whatever a philosopher may pretend, are acknowledged to be above the talents of common men.[43]

What we do not 'understand' we may still believe, and act on. The 'truth' of our religious utterances rests in their evoking and maintaining the 'cordial consent of beings to Being in general', their being such propositions as 'make proper impressions on [our] mind producing therein love, hope, gratitude, influencing [our] life and actions, agreeably to that notion of saving faith which is required in a Christian'.[44] This is not to adopt a post-modern, anti-realist stance: only to accept that this – if orthodox theism is correct – is the last best test of truth. The way of action may be more demanding, and more fruitful, than the way of knowledge.

It is reasonable to believe what we cannot 'prove'; it is even reasonable to believe, and feel, what we can't understand. Both theses depend upon a further 'religious' axiom, that the Origin is to be trusted. If we could not sensibly believe the testimony of ages, nor trust our common sense or 'natural taste', we should have no escape from chaos. To that extent, we *must* live on faith. If we could not sensibly believe that what is now obscure may still have a solution, and may guide our hearts, we must remain '*minute* philosophers'.[45] 'This being the case, how can it be questioned what course a wise man should take? Whether the principles of Christians or infidels are truest may be made a question; but which are safest can be none.'[46] Those who are moved neither by the past nor by the hope of a future that they don't yet understand have nothing to sustain or occupy them but their present pains or pleasures. We had better at least pretend that testimony can be relied on, that our thoughts aren't limited to what we now perceive, and that we can properly predict our futures on the basis of our remembered past.

A merely traditional believer might conclude that everything I have been saying is either unnecessary or else pernicious. If there is nothing wrong in being part of a community of faith (since none of us, whatever our particular faith may be, can ever quite escape in any case), then there is no need to 'prove' the essential theorems of a philosophical theism. Indeed, there is something wrong with the attempt: trying to *prove* them might suggest that there are other, better beliefs endorsed by another, rival community, while the whole point of religion is to be loyal to our own. Intellectuals who busily seek to 'prove' what their fellows already, rightly, know are only trying to elevate themselves above the common stock of justified belief. The very fact that they need to may suggest that they have some very basic flaw. The thought is not absurd. Amongst the ordinary, right beliefs of almost all (but not all) human communities are the following: there has been a world of much this sort for longer than one's personal memory; there are other people, with their own memories, intentions, feelings; material objects are not discontinuous. Someone who felt it necessary to 'prove' that other people had feelings would be a suspected psychopath, especially once it became clear that any such proofs that did establish the conclusion would instead destabilize the premises. Why may not the credal statements of religious sects be taken as equally basic: ones not requiring, nor allowing, proof, and yet being rightly believed by members of that sect? Granted that the very same theorem may seem obvious to one, and wholly suspect to another: what does that show except that only the former is a member of the relevant sect, church or community? We find what sect we are members of by realizing what we recognize as true.

But isn't there a problem? Orwell's O'Brien denied, like Wittgensteinians, that it was solipsistic to rely on what the community of faith should say: 'Collective solipsism, if you like. But that is a different thing: in fact the opposite thing.'[47] Clearly, there can be no such real distinction if there are no real individuals: where the only real or important thing is the Party, and the Party determines truth, that is solipsism, even if it differs from the more familiar kind. If Winston had successfully retreated to his own mind and memory, denying that anything could be true but what seemed so to him, then Ingsoc and O'Brien would call him solipsist: 'You are mentally deranged. You suffer from a defective memory. You are unable to remember real events and you persuade yourself that you remember other events which never happened.'[48] But O'Brien's claim is only and entirely in the name of the Party-Self: it is not that there is any *fact* outside, or anything that rests on more than what that Party-Self (in all its avatars) will say. Winston's 'delusion' is only his failure to submerge his trivial self in the larger whole. Personal memory and conviction are insufficient to establish truth: after all, Winston '*knew* ... that O'Brien was on his side ...'[49], 'knew instinctively who would survive and who would perish',[50] knew that he would not betray Julia as certainly as 'he knew the rules of arithmetic',[51] and his dreams are – in the story – much better predictors than his careful theories.[52] Only the public record serves – but that record is indefinitely manipulable. 'All the confessions uttered here are true. We make them true.'[53] Collective solipsism, and generalized anti-realism, are only the 'opposite' of solipsism in the way that one egoism is the opposite of another. It is not Winston that is the only real, but Big Brother:

> 'Does Big Brother exist?' 'Of course he exists. The Party exists. Big Brother is the embodiment of the Party.' 'Does he exist in the same way as I exist?' 'You do not exist,' said O'Brien.[54]

We must retain the axiom that it is Truth (God, Being) that should determine what we say, and not the community, nor any finite being. We can agree that our own thoughts most probably derive from just such a community, and that any individual challenge is a risk. But any such community that denies the possibility of revelation, or of reason, is corrupt. Most prophets may be false prophets: every sect that silences the prophets has also left the way. Once again, theism seems the safest option.

NINE

THE LAST THINGS

Inexpugnable Realism

ACCORDING TO LOVEJOY,

the primary and most universal faith of man [is] his inexpugnable realism, his twofold belief that he is on the one hand in the midst of realities which are not himself nor mere obsequious shadows of himself, a world which transcends the narrow confines of his own transient being; and on the other hand that he can himself somehow read beyond those confines and bring those external existences within the compass of his own life yet without annulment of their transcendence.[1]

The religion that we need at this tail-end of twentieth-century progress is one that allows us to acknowledge the reality, the beauty, the demands of Truth, without despairing of success or putting too much of our trust in easy victories. We need to be able, honestly, to believe that we can find things out about the way things work, and that we should do – but that 'the way things work' is only part of Truth.[2] We need to be able to believe that the world is not entirely alien, and that it is not entirely ours. Traditional theistic religion provides the texts, the creeds, the rituals and ceremonials within which we can find that balance.

There is as good reason to believe its claims as to believe the claims of 'science', since science (historically and philosophically) depends on something indistinguishable from realistic theism. There is as good reason to honour God as to honour any real virtue, for ethical virtue (historically and philosophically) depends on the belief that something really matters, and that we are not in the end deceived. Those who denounce the essence of traditional religion – and not just its frequent errors – are in error. 'The modern schemes of our free-thinkers, who pretend to separate morality from religion, how rational soever they seem to their admirers, are in truth and effect, most irrational and pernicious to civil society.'[3] If theism were not true, there would be no truth worth attending to, or accessible to us, beyond our immediate sensations. On those terms, there would of course be nothing wrong in playing games, pretending to believe in God as well as Santa Claus: insofar as pretended atheists insist that Truth is worth pursuing, and can sometimes be caught, they fail to recognize the implications of their own belief.

Those who 'separate morality from religion' may sometimes, high-mindedly, insist that they alone are true believers in the moral realm: theists, they say, only do what's right because they fear their Maker. Such moral realism is unstable: without some notion of the infinite and omnipresent Being it is unclear what sort of being 'moral rules' can have, or how we could come to know them. Few such modern moralists are Platonists, affirming the eternal being of real standards – and Platonists, of course, concluded (as above) that such standards were the eternal thoughts of God. Atheistical moralists have no clear account of what eternal standards could be, nor any account of how they might affect the world. As Mackie pointed out, if there is no causal link between the standards and our belief in them, then we must conclude that we would feel the same whatever those 'objective standards' were. From this it follows that we don't need to postulate them. Morality, in God's absence, soon becomes a set of agreed rules and gestures. Even this is less secure than atheistic moralists suppose: why should we ever expect that there could be a universal agreement such that everyone, or even every rational creature, would be content with just those rules? It is a theistic hope that there will be a day, the Day of the Lord, when everyone agrees. Without that hope what reason could we have to think that there is only one, or even one, such set of rationally agreed procedures? It follows that 'morality' could only be a chance-met set of rules, accepted – briefly – by one set of creatures. Communities conflict, and nothing ties us even to one community. Even those moralists who argue that species-survival is an absolute are bound to be in error: species diverge into new species; even while they last they are no more than sets of interbreeding populations. Nothing says that everyone, or anyone, will put the interests (what are they?) of species-progeny above their own, or aliens'. Why should they?

Once again: if there is no God, there are no absolute standards of right and wrong, and therefore no reason to complain when others have invented them. Even if (absurdly) there were no truth, we would be best advised to think there was: those who say there isn't, or that we shouldn't thus pretend, are talking – as so often – nonsense. As Chesterton put it:

> Do you think I have no right to fight for Notting Hill, you whose English Government has so often fought for tomfooleries? If, as your rich friends say, there are no gods, and the skies are dark above us, what should a man fight for but the place where he had the Eden of childhood and the short heaven of first love? If no temples and no scriptures are sacred, what is sacred if a man's own youth is not sacred?[4]

Orwell's imagined future also uses war to bind the hearts and minds of its subjects, and upholds the importance of what 'we' say against 'mere facts'. The differences are that Chesterton's common men are replaced by Orwell's proles, and there is no 'last, lost giant, even God' to rise against the world.[5] A man's youth is *not* sacred, nor is childhood remotely like Eden. 'Hardly a week passed in which *The Times* did not carry a paragraph describing how some eavesdropping little sneak – 'child hero' was the phrase generally used – had overheard some compromising remark and denounced its parents to the Thought Police.'[6] Rorty asks:

> Suppose that Socrates was wrong, that we have *not* once seen the Truth, and so will not, intuitively, recognize it when we see it again. This means that when the secret police come, when the torturers violate the innocent, there is nothing to be said to them of the form 'There is something within you which you are betraying. Though you embody the practices of a totalitarian society which will endure forever, there is something beyond those practices which condemns you.'[7]

Suppose instead that Socrates was right.

Objects, Projects, Revelations

Modernity is dominated by the doctrine that the world is made of 'objects', things to be understood as moved by mechanistic laws. Since we are ourselves supposed to be amongst those objects, we must conceive ourselves to be moved only in such ways, and not by any sense of epistemic or ethical right or wrong. Since it is supremely difficult for us to retain just that 'objective' look at our own preferences and policies, the urge to treat 'all things' as objects generally means, in practice, that we treat them only as means to our own ends (which are somehow exempted from the objectifying gaze). Some critics, blaming our current crisis on that simple-minded greed, have urged us instead to realize that the world is made of things like us – namely with inner feelings. To grasp the world, they say, we need to revert to 'animistic' or projective methods, purged of the grosser forms of self-deceit, but nonetheless owing more to romantic poetry than 'science'.

As I argued in a previous chapter, pantheism, whether romantic or philosophical, is precisely not what we need to believe in if we are to solve our crisis. Objectifying science has been a necessary discipline. It is so easy to allow our fancies to infect our recognition of Reality, that we had better, for a while, reject all forms of projective, participatory understanding. It is so easy to confuse what *we* think ought to be the case with what we have good reason to think is the case (and this in turn with what actually is), that we had better separate Fact and Value in our thoughts. It does not follow that there are no real values, nor that participatory understanding, purified, is not a vital part of decent thought. We ought to try to be genuinely objective precisely because the Real, the Actual, the True, imposes obligations on us. We *ought* to try to see things as they are, and not simply as we are told they are, or as we would wish them to be. We *ought* to follow where Nature leads: at any rate in this sense, that we ought to say and think that Being Is, and that we know it is, and that we are ourselves at once a part of it, and faced by it. In thus submitting to Fact we bind ourselves at least to hope for the same confidence that Augustine expressed:

I am confident that God in His mercy will make me steadfast in all the truths which I regard as certain, but if I am minded otherwise in any point, He Himself will make it known to me, either by His own secret inspirations, or through His own lucid words, or through discussions with my brethren. For this I do pray, and I place this trust and this desire in His hands, who is wholly capable of guarding what He has given and of fulfilling what He has promised.[8]

And now suppose that orthodox, historical, personalistic theism genuinely is true. It is better to think of Truth as Someone than as Something. The demand we – mostly – recognize, to bow to Truth, is at that Someone's urging. Realists all admit they might be wrong, and wish they weren't. Theists pray to be enlightened by the truth – and also recognize that, much of the time, we don't really want to be shocked out of our pretences. 'Wickedness makes us lie about the principles of our actions', about what we mean to do.[9] Knowing that we are easily deceived (and love to be deceived) we sometimes have the grace to pray for refutation.

How would such a God refute us, or communicate with us? Philosophers will usually prefer to hope that God's word will be revealed in reason. What we seriously and disinterestedly come to hold, on the basis of clear and distinct proposals acceptable to critical intelligence, will be our guide to Heaven's Gate. Unfortunately, we are well aware that all our thoughts are fragmentary, our thinking flawed. Even if the being and nature of God were evident to reason we could hardly hope to learn them: we have occasional glimpses of what 'reason' would involve, but by those very glimpses know how far we are from reason. We need to believe that truth is possible for us, but recognize that we could not – believably – construct it. Reason tells us that there are things *we* cannot learn by reason. 'There might be patterns of [belief or] unbelief that we are particularly prone toward, or thoughts we constantly avoid because of "the smoke of our wrong-doing", to use St. Anselm's colorful phrase.'[10] Faced by the Infinite and Eternal even angels, who are pure intellects, may tremble: what hope have we?

Abrahamic theism, in its various guises, has chosen or been chosen to insist that God has addressed us on particular occasions: has told us things we could not have expected. God so conceived surpasses any reasoned object of religion – but of course the pagan theist also held that God surpassed our reason, and inspired the fortunate. God has set *nous*, the intuitive intellect, as a fire in our souls.[11] There are truths we cannot work out for ourselves. The only question is: does God tell everyone, or everyone that's human, or that's wise? Perhaps He plants His messages, His spirit, elsewhere than the self-styled wise expect. Pagans – by and large – believed that God would only befriend the best and wisest of us – but they also suspected that 'becoming wise' could only be a gift of God, a sudden and unprecedented transformation. Would the wise do this or that? Who knows, not being wise, what they would do? Pagan commentators on the Hebrew scriptures usually believed that they could, after all, distinguish what was universal, moral duty from parochial or superstitious rite. How else could any scripture show it was from God except by saying what we already 'know' God says? And why, if that is all it says, should anyone need to read it?

The converse claim is that we actually know very little of what God would say, and need to be informed. Maybe it would be better to assume, at first, that the scriptures are from God, and only at last reject them if they certainly fall foul of sounder revelation. Certainly, the Stoics themselves were willing to argue that God would not leave us without witnesses, and hence that we could pick up unexpected truths from unreasoning places.[12] Certainly, we are not ourselves so wise as wisely to disdain the common maxims. The God of Abraham is the God of the Philosophers, and sensible philosophers must think it possible that they have things to learn even from unphilosophical theists. More than possible: we actually need to realize that God and His Commandments are not spun out of our own reasonings (and therefore must sometimes be unexpected). A god that said all and only what I expect, could only be a figment (or a demon): it follows that nothing can be God who does not startle me, and that it would be correspondingly absurd to disregard such startling revelations. Our devotion as good philosophers must be to Truth, not simply to what we think is true – although we cannot turn aside from what we *think* is true to Truth itself except by miracle.

And what of 'science', and the specious claim that 'scientists' have learned to dispense with deity, that 'God' is an unnecessary hypothesis? In fact the very claim that we ought only to believe what is confirmed by mathematical reason and experimental evidence only makes sense if theism is true. What other metaphysic makes it even possible that a chance-bred talent for tracking wildebeest or telling stories will turn out to be a route to wisdom? Science rests upon the unproven and – in the abstract – ludicrous conviction that the world is one, that it runs by mathematical formulae which we can discover, that it will prove to be worth knowing. Historically and philosophically it rests on theism. If, *per impossibile*, it could prove theism false, it would have lost its credibility. The Death of God is followed by the death of knowledge. Theologians, accordingly, have no need to speak so softly. Once upon a time, some theologians rejected heliocentrism (not because they thought the Earth was too important to be a satellite, but because they doubted that 'science' could or should be taken as a guide to how things 'really' were). Perhaps they were in error (though it is now a commonplace that scientists don't tell us 'how it is' but 'how it's sensible to speak of it'). Once upon a rather later time, some theologians expressed some hesitation about Darwin's theory of natural selection (doubts almost all scientific or moral in their origin, not theological). There have been plenty of other occasions when well-educated theists were the ones to maintain some truth in the face of scientific fashion (the unity, for example, of humankind, or the absurdity of eugenicism). We should not abandon fundamental truths: that there is a real truth accessible to human reason which we should pursue. We should not allow ourselves to be infected by any aphorisms incompatible with that real truth, which is indeed 'religious': the rituals are required to help us to remember it, and feel its influence in our lives.

Ethics and Immortality

It is appropriate at this point to return yet again to the 'ethical' interpretation of theism. Simple anti-realists may say that 'the existence of God' rests only in 'our' determination to be 'godly'. Unfortunately, a command I issue to myself has neither power nor authority to bind me against my actual will – and hence is no command at all. Moral realists who 'disbelieve in God' insist that there are 'real' moral truths outside of our intention. Unfortunately, if those truths have no real causal power we must conclude that we believe in them because of what we are, and not because of what they are: it follows that any belief we have in them is one we could and would have even if we were entirely wrong about them (and hence can never be justified). The choice is simple: either moral realists will swiftly become anti-realists instead, or else they must admit that 'moral truths' have causal power (that is, they must admit the truth of metaphysical theism).[13] And any realist, agreeing that the truth of what we justly believe does not rest in our agreement to it (or even our finding it intuitively plausible), must accept that some ethical demands (some moral truths) will not be what we hoped for.[14]

Chesterton, whom I have cited so often in this study, wrote a great deal, and often far too rapidly: like Plotinus, and like the journalist he was proud to be, he did not go in for revisions.[15] Some critical comment is extraordinarily lumbering and obtuse, but occasionally even an admirer must admit that he has erred: many of the Father Brown stories are too obviously designed to make a point against a modern habit. 'The Invisible Man', for example,[16] turns on the suggestion that no one would notice that the postman had been, because we cannot see the human person underneath the 'striking and even showy costume' of red, blue and gold. Actually there can be few more noticeable persons than a postman: 'who can bear to feel himself forgotten?'[17] Even if we do not often engage tradesmen and civil servants in lengthy conversation, we certainly know they are there. Chesterton exaggerated (or rather spoke falsely) because he wanted to indict the 'modern' world for errors regularly attributed to the pre-modern, of confusing person and station, and denying human reality to the working poor. Though he was wrong in detail, he may been right in principle – actually in two principles. First, he was right to point out the 'contextuality' of questions: 'people never answer what you say: they answer what you mean – or what they think you mean'[18] – so that witnesses might honestly insist that 'no man has gone into the Mansions' meaning merely that 'no man whom they could suspect of being your man' had gone in. Second, he was right to point out the existence of 'social invisibility' – a phenomenon of which John Braintree (the Labour spokesman in *The Return of Don Quixote*) also complains to one who has said that there are no men around at all (of a kind judged suitable to take part in amateur dramatics):

> There is a man in the next room, there is a man in the passage; there is a man in the garden; there is a man at the front door; there is a man in the stables; there is a man in the kitchen; there is a man in the cellar. What sort of palace of lies have you built for yourselves, when you see all these around you every day and do not even know that they are men? Why do we strike? Because you forget our very existence when we do not strike.'[19]

Our own age is not immune. As I write, large areas of the Caribbean island of Montserrat have been evacuated for fear of a further volcanic eruption: 'no one is left living there' – except of course uncounted wild things, cattle, and domestic dogs left chained to wait their death. Accustomed language governs thought: what is needed is the sudden realization of something that transcends such custom.

The recognition of such real creatures, and the associated conviction that God wishes them to be, lies at the root of ethical respect – and also of belief in immortality. To value something is to wish that it exist, and therefore to wish that it exist forever. At one level, this seems silly, or even sinful. It is quite clear that every finite creature perishes, and it is fairly easy, in the abstract, to convince oneself that wishing a longer life, let alone immortal life, to anything is wishing away its own particular charm. Wanting something to live longer than its 'natural term' would be like wanting it to be much larger than it is. Why should a longer duration be more desirable than a larger waist band? On this account, admiring recognition of a creature's being must entail our wishing it to last, in time, no longer than it 'naturally should'. We can of course confirm that feeling in ourselves by recollecting all the losses, pains, embarrassments that go along with age. Wishing a long life to someone may be wishing them a lengthy death. If, on the other hand, we wish them *health* forever (however unrealistically), we may be wishing them to be a different sort of thing entirely. A creature gifted with unending youth will be a very different sort of creature from our present selves. How could we recognize them in a thousand, or ten thousand, or a million years? A human being condemned to live that long would have no closer connection to 'her own' early youth than to any other of her first contemporaries.[20]

So one conclusion – and perhaps the right one – would be that a proper attitude to life, and Truth, demands a rational acceptance of defining limits. Mayflies, to be mayflies, live a day: people live for three-score years and ten, and if by reason of strength we achieve four-score yet is our strength but labour and sorrow. A further twist might add that God, the Truth, contains all proper beings: the Truth is unchangeable, and every creature it sustains retains its being – but only as the being it is. Imagine that the fantasy of time-travel is real: then we can conclude that nothing is ever lost. A time-traveller can revisit any creature:

> Fair youth, beneath the trees, thou canst not leave
> Thy song, nor ever can those trees be bare;
> Bold lover, never, never canst thou kiss,
> Though winning near the goal – yet, do not grieve;
> She cannot fade, though thou hast not thy bliss,
> For ever wilt thou love, and she be fair![21]

Maybe that is the rational conclusion. But it is also possible to believe that there may be a higher destiny: not simply to last for centuries, or 'forever', in the life one lived; nor yet to see that life extended, artificially, till it is no more one life than any other's. The promise Abrahamic theists hold is that the being of those we love will be, and is, exalted. The beings they are 'in God' are different from what they would have been if they had never been unfolded into the world of pain and time and chance. Each being Here is, as it were, the seed of something infinite: a portrait, or a vision, of the One, True Infinite, and therefore bound to be forever. Maybe our 'rational' conclusion that each creature has a limit, beyond which it either must decay or change into a radically different thing, has too low a view. To value something is to wish that it exist: but what we wish depends on our conception of that thing. In loving Beatrice, Dante saw the possibility, or else the eternal fact, of Beatrice Exalted: someone of whom *his* vision of Beatrice – or Beatrice's vision of Beatrice – was no more than a sketch, or shadow.

The connection between this mortal body and the exalted being is not subject to calculation of the sort that analytical philosophers have tried. Beatrice Exalted and the young girl Dante met in Florence are 'the same', but not because the former has the latter's memories or vital parts. The person variously seen in Florence (who died young) was the outward, mortal copy of the real being. The very life of time is only a copy or a shadow of eternal life, which may, at times, break in on us. It may also, somehow, contribute some value to that life.

This aspect of most Abrahamic faith, a belief in resurrection, is not, perhaps, entailed by basic theistic tenets. Maybe God contains, for each of us, no more than the lives we manage to live here-now. Maybe there is no resurrection, nor any 'eternal life' beyond the timeless life of Keats's Urn. Maybe, on the other hand, there will be something like a 'literal resurrection', when we'll be restored to better lives than this, for ever, in a world that can be understood in much the same way as this present world. If we can fantasize that future science will one day reconstruct us (and some science fantasists – not only science fiction writers – do just that), it isn't difficult to think that the Omnipotent could do the same. But such a 'literal resurrection' to a life much like the present (but, obviously, better) is neither required by theists, nor desired. It is raised a *spiritual* body. It doesn't follow that a merely 'anti-realist' or ethical interpretation of the resurrection into life eternal is appropriate. If orthodox theists are correct each of us, all being well, will rise to life eternal. We shall all be changed. Haldane was right, in a way, in one thing: 'a good Christian would feel himself insulted by the suggestion that his life was limited to such a period [as the inconceivably vast expanse of 10^{googol} years].'[22] Because God loves what He has made, it is indeed forever.

Pagan theists generally believed that only 'the wise' could really be God's friends, and only the wise, if they, could hope to share His life. Jews, Christians and Muslims disagree: none of us are *wise*, but all of us are God's. 'The mere fact that we exist proves [God's] infinite and eternal love, for from all eternity he chose us from among an infinite number of possible beings.'[23] Every thing we meet is also chosen: that is a good enough reason not to despise or hurt it. Whether it will be a strong enough reason to prevent us, I do not know. God knows. But if God chooses us to be, we can expect that He chooses us to be forever, by whatever means He chooses.

Julian of Norwich records that God showed her

> a little thing, the size of a hazel-nut, on the palm of [her] hand, round like a ball. [She] looked at it thoughtfully and wondered, 'What is this?' And the answer came, 'It is all that is made.' [She] marvelled that it continued to exist and did not suddenly disintegrate; it was so small. And again [her] mind supplied the answer, 'It exists, both now and for ever, because God loves it.' In short, everything owes its existence to the love of God.'[24]

Looking beyond the World

Judaism, though there have been times and places when it sought a wider audience, is not at present an 'ecumenical' religion. The people of Israel are indeed a people, united by family ties, shared histories of persecution and success, as well as by defining rituals. 'Believing in God', for many Israelites, is only being committed to some version, more or less severe, of their ancestral custom. It doesn't matter what God *is*, but rather what a good Jew is. That way of life has long outlasted empires, and there is a strong, historical case for saying that the present, human world is governed by ideals that first took shape in Israel – even when those ideals are overtly atheistic. A theological realist may well conclude that God is keeping His promises. The people has survived, and all the nations of the world owe Abraham.

Other Abrahamic groups have more obviously global aims, and seek to influence the masters of the world. There may be many points on which Christians and Muslims (in particular) agree, while disagreeing just as strongly with Communists and Liberals alike. Unfortunately, both these global creeds have their own ethnic or parochial associations. Christians are seen (despite the spread of 'Third World Christianity') as Westerners; Muslims are seen (despite the longterm presence of Islam as far as Iran and Indonesia) as Arabs. Both groups have a long imperial past: medieval Christians had as powerful reasons to distrust Islam as modern Muslims have to distrust the West. Some small groups, inevitably, seek to compromise, or find the shared essentials of all 'great religions'. It seems, unfortunately, likely that such sects will be regarded as heretical, and rarely influence more than intellectuals. Religions prosper when they shape a people – and peoples always find themselves opposed to other peoples they despise or fear.

If theism is correct, there is a power which will amend our ways. But nothing in tradition shows that It will do so as we choose It should. Modern religiosity has tended to expect some gradual 'improvements' in material or moral circumstance (just as our predecessors, with as firm a conviction, expected to deteriorate). Earlier ages have suspected that theirs was the last age of the world. Obviously, they were mistaken – but they were not foolish in suspecting it. Oddly, although we have far stronger reason to suspect that our age is the last one, we believe, without much argument, that only fools will say the end is nigh. That prophecy has so often been disproved that we assume it will be yet again.

But there is good reason after all for every generation of humanity to suspect that theirs might be the last, or at least the largest.[25] Suppose we knew that there were a string of rooms, each larger than the last, and holding fifty, five hundred, five thousand, fifty thousand (and so on for no one knows how long) human beings. Suppose that you were placed, blindfold, in one room or another: where should you bet you were? Plainly, the chances are that you are in the largest room, so that you have good reason to suspect that there are no larger rooms than whatever room in which you find yourself. Again: if people ascend from here to occupy the galaxies, it will turn out that you and I are astonishingly early humans. Almost every human who ever lives will live long after us. Isn't it more rational to suspect that we are not early, that we already occupy the centuries when almost all the people who have ever lived will live? Isn't that more rational especially when, for the first time ever, we actually have the power to bring things to an end? The pessimistic thought afflicting those inclined to wonder about other thinking peoples, elsewhere in the universe, is that such thinking peoples almost always perish long before they can make their presence known.[26]

This is, it seems, the rational conclusion: not that we are *bound* to perish, but that we should give that outcome a far higher initial probability, and worry a lot more about the risks we run. That is also the witness of Scripture: the Day of the Lord is not the culmination of a gradual improvement, but the Day when debts are called in, and a reckoning made. Why should we have expected otherwise? 'Yahweh describes himself [in the Book of Job] as the wisdom that makes for the survival of the wild ass, the hamster, the eagle, the ostrich, or all living nature, and the wisdom that uproots mountains and annihilates angels.'[27] God can raise new peoples (*laoi*) from the stones (*laes*), and being called to be 'human' is a new vocation, not a destiny, nor what the worlds were made for.[28] If we smugly believed that God was bound to want things just like us, and made a sidereal universe solely as the only way to get what He wanted – we were, on theological as well as neo-Darwinian grounds, mistaken. We are utterly dependent on what we call God: piety consists in recognizing that dependence, and our consanguinity with all the things that share in being with us. Everything is an end in itself; nothing only a means. Everything is an epiphany; nothing is to be mistaken for the One, not even our own best image of that One.

Whether or not the Last Days are upon us, we can still be sure that each of us will die: that is the other axiom of rational religion, alongside the hope of eternal life. We can also, on past form, be confident that we will be forgotten in this world, 'as if we had never been', by coming generations. Even those whose names survive in history can be sure that nothing much reliable will last, and that whatever they once thought they had accomplished will dissolve (and they are best remembered, if at all, for something they had not intended). There have of course been some occasional accomplishments that lasted, or were remembered. Even they cannot be guaranteed to have increased the sum of human or any other happiness over what might have been. Most of us will accomplish no such thing. Whatever we do, or undo, will make no lasting difference.

Or is that downbeat judgement a deception? We will be forgotten, yes: but does it follow that our acts have no effects?

May we not be coming closer to a time when it is not just every Israelite (as the Talmud says) but every human creature that holds the honour of their people in their hands?

What we accomplish, often against our conscious wishes and without our knowledge, must be, if theists are right, by God's grace and permission. Whatever purpose it is that He is working out is not confined to this world here, and the effects He desires may not be manifested here. It does not follow – as some have thought – that theists have no interest in looking after 'the material world', as though it were mere material. On the contrary, if we can't love the beings that we do see, how can we love 'the Father', whom we don't? To love the Father is to endorse His choice. But the direction of a theist's care must always be a little different: we must act as the God whom I have been describing would, and does, command. The goal cannot be merely a long life, nor yet to have amassed possessions, reputation or accomplishments. In Augustine's words: 'I had promised to show you, if you recall, that there is something higher than our mind and reason. There you have it – truth itself! Embrace it if you can and enjoy it.'[29]

Our duty as theists is to enjoy the truth, and therefore to take 'the simple, unasking pleasure in the existence of other creatures that is possible to humans'.[30] Taking that pleasure in the world God makes we uncover something that will be forever: God's pleasure in the things He makes is their own wish to be. The former is eternal: so also the latter.

WORKS CITED

Anscombe, G. E. M., *Metaphysics and the Philosophy of Mind*, Blackwell, Oxford, 1981

Apuleius, *The Isis-Book*, ed. J. G. Griffiths, Brill, Leiden, 1975

Atkins, P., *The Creation*, Freeman, Oxford, 1981

Auden, W. H., *Collected Shorter Poems 1926–56*, Faber, London, 1966

Augustine, *On Christian Doctrine*, tr. D. W. Robertson, Bobbs-Merrill, Indianapolis, 1958

Augustine, *Confessions*, tr. R. S. Pine-Coffin, Harmondsworth, Penguin, 1961

Augustine, *The Trinity*, tr. S. McKenna, Catholic University of America Press, Washington, 1963

Augustine, *The Teacher, The Free Choice of the Will & Grace and Free Will*, tr. R. P. Russell, Catholic University of America Press, Washington, 1968

Ayer, A. J., *Language, Truth and Logic*, Gollancz, London, 1946 (2nd edn)

Berkeley, G., *Collected Works*, eds. A. A. Luce & T. E. Jessop, Thomas Nelson, Edinburgh, 1948–56

Berry, W., *What are People For?*, Rider Books, London, 1991 (first published 1990)

Blake, W., *Collected Works*, ed. G. Keynes, Oxford University Press, London, 1966

Boethius, *Tractates & Consolation of Philosophy*, tr. H. F. Stewart, E. K. Rand, S. J. Tester, Heinemann Loeb Classical Library, London, 1973

Boswell, J., *Life of Johnson*, Oxford University Press, London, 1953

Buchan, J., *The Moon Endureth*, Thomas Nelson, Edinburgh, 1923

Cardenal, E., *Love*, tr. D. Livingstone, Search Press, London, 1974

Chandrasekhar, S., *Truth and Beauty*, University of Chicago Press, Chicago, 1987

Chesterton, G. K., *A Short History of England*, Chatto & Windus, London, 1917

Chesterton, G. K. (1923a), *Fancies versus Fads*, Methuen, London, 1923

Chesterton, G. K. (1923b), *St. Francis of Assisi*, Hodder & Stoughton, London, 1923

Chesterton, G. K., *The Everlasting Man*, Hodder & Stoughton, London, 1925

Chesterton, G. K., *The Return of Don Quixote*, Chatto & Windus, London, 1927

Chesterton, G. K., *The Father Brown Stories*, Cassell, London, 1929

Chesterton, G. K., *Chaucer*, Faber, London, 1932

Chesterton, G. K., *St Thomas Aquinas*, Hodder & Stoughton, London, 1933

Chesterton, G. K., *The Man who was Thursday*, Penguin, Harmondsworth, 1937 (first published 1908)

Chesterton, G. K., *The Napoleon of Notting Hill*, Penguin, Harmondsworth, 1946 (first published 1904)

Chesterton, G. K., *Manalive*, Penguin, Harmondsworth, 1947 (first published 1912)

Chesterton, G. K., *Collected Poems*, Methuen, London, 1950

Chesterton, G. K., *Orthodoxy*, Fontana, London, 1961 (first published 1908)

Chesterton, G. K., *The Poet and the Lunatics*, Darwen Finlayson, London, 1962 (1st edn 1949)

Clark, S. R. L., 'God, good and evil': *Proceedings of the Aristotelian Society* 77.1977, pp. 247ff

Clark, S. R. L., 'The lack of a gap between Fact and Value': *Aristotelian Society Supplementary* Vol. 54.1980, pp. 245ff

Clark, S. R. L., 'God's Law and Morality': *Philosophical Quarterly* 32.1982, pp. 339–47

Clark, S. R. L., *From Athens to Jerusalem*, Clarendon Press, Oxford, 1984

Clark, S. R. L., 'God's Law and Chandler': *Philosophical Quarterly* 37.1987, pp. 200–206

Clark, S. R. L. (1989a), *Civil Peace and Sacred Order*, Clarendon Press, Oxford, 1989

Clark, S. R. L. (1989b), 'Mackie and the Moral Order': *Philosophical Quarterly* 39.1989, pp. 98–144

Clark, S. R. L., *A Parliament of Souls*, Clarendon Press, Oxford, 1990

Clark, S. R. L., *God's World and the Great Awakening*, Clarendon Press, Oxford, 1991

Clark, S. R. L. (1992a), 'Descartes' Debt to Augustine': M. McGhee, ed., *Philosophy, Religion and the Spiritual Life* (Cambridge University Press 1992), pp. 73–88

Clark, S. R. L. (1992b), 'Orwell and the Anti-Realists': *Philosophy* 67.1992, pp. 141–54

Clark, S. R. L. (1992c), 'Where have all the Angels gone?': *Religious Studies* 28.1992, pp. 221–34

Clark, S. R. L. (1993a), *How to Think about the Earth: models of environmental theology*, Scott-Holland lectures at Liverpool 1992, Mowbrays, London, 1993

Clark, S. R. L. (1993b), 'Natural Goods and Moral Beauty': D. Knowles & J. Skorupski, eds., *Virtue and Taste: Essays on politics, ethics and aesthetics in memory of Flint Schier* (Blackwell: Oxford 1993), pp. 83–97

Clark, S. R. L. (1993c), 'The Better Part': A. Phillips-Griffiths, ed., *Ethics* (Cambridge University Press: Cambridge 1993), pp. 29–49

Clark, S. R. L., 'Extraterrestrial Intelligence, the Neglected Experiment': *Foundation* 61.1994, pp. 50–65

Clark, S. R. L., *How to Live Forever* (1995a), Routledge, London, 1995

Clark, S. R. L. (1995b), 'Objective Values, Final Causes': *Electronic Journal of Analytical Philosophy* 3.1995, pp. 65–78 (http://www.phil.indiana. edu/ejap/)

Clark, S. R. L. (1995c), 'Substance, or Chesterton's Abyss of Light': *Proceedings of the Aristotelian Society Supplementary volume* 95. 1995, pp. 1–14

Clark, S. R. L.,'Plotinus: Body and Mind' (1996a): *Cambridge Companion to Plotinus*, ed. L. Gerson (Cambridge University Press: Cambridge 1996), pp. 275–91

Clark, S. R. L. (1996b), 'How Chesterton Read History': *Inquiry* 39.1996, pp. 343–58

Clark, S. R. L., 'A Plotinian Account of Intellect': *American Catholic Philosophical Journal* 71.1997, pp. 421–32

Clark, S. R. L., 'Pantheism': David E. Cooper & Joy A. Palmer, eds., *Spirit of the Environment* (Routledge: London 1998), pp. 42–56

Clark, S. R. L.,'Berkeley's Philosophy of Religion': Kenneth Winckler, ed., *Companion to Berkeley* (Cambridge: Cambridge University Press), forthcoming

Clark, S. R. L., 'How and Why to be Virtuous': *The Personalist Review*, forthcoming

Cotter, J. F., *Inscape: the Christology and Poetry of Hopkins*, University of Pittsburgh Press, Pittsburgh, 1972

Craig, W. L. *The* Kalam *Cosmological Argument*, Macmillan, London, 1979

Craig, W. L. & Smith, Q., *Theism, Atheism and Big Bang Cosmology*, Clarendon Press, Oxford, 1993

Cupitt, D., *Christ and the Hiddenness of God*, Lutterworth Press, London, 1971

Cupitt, D., *Taking Leave of God*, SCM Press, London, 1980

Cupitt, D., *Creation out of Nothing*, SCM Press, London, 1990

Dale, A. S., *The Outline of Sanity*, William B. Eerdmans, Grand Rapids, 1982

Darwin, C., *The Descent of Man*, Princeton University Press, Princeton, 1981 (reprint of 1st edn, 1871)

Dawkins, R., *The Blind Watchmaker*, Longman Scientific & Technical, Harlow, 1986

Descartes, R., *Philosophical Works*, eds., E. S. Haldane & G. R. T. Ross, Cambridge University Press, Cambridge, 1931

Descartes, R., *Philosophical Letters*, ed. A. Kenny, Oxford University Press, Oxford, 1970

Descartes, R. *Principles of Philosophy*, tr. V. R. Miller & R. P. Miller, Reidel, Dordrecht & Boston, 1983

Diels, H. & Krantz, W., eds., *Die Fragmente der Vorsokratiker*, Berlin, 1952 (6th edition)

Dodds, E. R., *Pagan and Christian in an Age of Anxiety*, Cambridge University Press, Cambridge, 1965

Dostoyevsky, F. M., *Letters to Family and Friends*, tr. E. C. Mayne, Chatto & Windus, London, 1962

Eco, U., *Art and Beauty in the Middle Ages*, tr. H. Bredin, Yale University Press, New Haven and London, 1986

Edwards, J., *Basic Writings*, ed. O. E. Winslow, New American Library, New York, 1966

Epictetus, *Discourses and Encheiridion*, tr. W. A. Oldfather, Heinemann Loeb Classical Library, London, 1926

Evans-Pritchard, E., *Nuer Religion*, Clarendon Press, Oxford, 1956

Fox, M., *The Coming of the Cosmic Christ*, Harper & Row, New York, 1988

Gardner, H., ed., *New Oxford Book of English Verse*, Clarendon Press, Oxford, 1972

Geach, P., 'What Actually Exists', *Proceedings of the Aristotelian Society, Supplementary Volume* 42.1968, pp. 7–16

Gleick, J., *Chaos: making a new science*, Penguin, Harmondsworth, 1987

Goddard, D., ed., *The Buddhist Bible*, Beacon Press, Boston, 1970

Haldane, E. S., *Descartes: his life and times*, John Murray, London, 1905

Haldane, J. B. S., *Possible Worlds and Other Essays*, Chatto & Windus, London, 1930 (first published 1927)

Haldane, J. B. S., *Fact and Faith*, Watts & Co, London, 1934

Heidegger, M., *What is Called Thinking?*, tr. J. Glenn Gray & F. Wieck, Harper & Row, New York, 1968

Herbert, Edward, *De Veritate*, tr. M. H. Carré, Arrowsmith, Bristol, 1937

Herbert, George, *Poems*, ed. H. Gardner, Oxford University Press, London, 1961

Holbrook, C. A., *The Ethics of Jonathan Edwards*, University of Michigan Press, Ann Arbor, 1973

Holscher, L., *The Reality of the Mind*, Routledge & Kegan Paul, London, 1986

Hopkins, G. M., *Journals and Papers*, eds., H. House & G. Storey, Oxford University Press, London, 1959

Hopkins, G. M., *Poems*, eds., W. H. Gardner & N. H. Mackenzie, Oxford University Press: London, 1967

Hopkins, J., *Nicholas of Cusa on Learned Ignorance*, Arthur J. Banning Press, Minneapolis, 1981

Hooykaas, R., *Religion and the Rise of Modern Science*, Scottish Academic Press, Edinburgh, 1972

Hume, D., *Hume on Religion*, ed. R. Wollheim, Fontana, London, 1963

Julian of Norwich, *Revelations of Divine Love*, tr. C. Wolters, Penguin, Harmondsworth, 1966

Kallen, H. M., 'The Book of Job as Greek Tragedy', N. N. Glatzer, ed., *The Dimensions of Job*, Schocken Books, New York, 1969, pp. 17ff

Keats, J., *Poetical Works*, ed., H. W. Garrod, Oxford University Press, London, 1956

Kenny, A., *The God of the Philosophers*, Clarendon Press, Oxford, 1979

Kirk, G. S., Raven, J. E. & Schofield, M., eds., *The Presocratic Philosophers*, Cambridge University Press, Cambridge, 1983

Konyndyk, Kenneth J., 'Aquinas on Faith and Science', *Faith and Philosophy* 12.1995, pp. 3–21

Lehrer, K., 'Why not Scepticism?', *Philosophical Forum* 2, 1970–1, pp. 283ff

Leslie, J., *The End of the World*, Routledge, London, 1996

Lewis, C. S., *That Hideous Strength*, Bodley Head, London, 1945

Lewis, C. S., *The Abolition of Man*, Bles, London, 1946 (2nd edn)

Lewis, C. S., *Miracles*, Bles, London, 1947; 2nd edn Fontana, London, 1960

London, J., *The Iron Heel*, Cooperative Publishing Society of Foreign Workers in the USSR, Moscow & Leningrad, 1934 (first published 1907)

Long, A. A. & Sedley, D. N., eds., *The Hellenistic Philosophers*, Cambridge University Press, Cambridge, 1987

Lossky, V., *The Mystical Theology of the Eastern Church*, James Clarke & Co, Cambridge, 1957

Lovejoy, A. O., *The Revolt against Dualism*, La Salle, Illinois, 1930

McDowell, J., 'Aesthetic value, objectivity and the fabric of the world', E. Schaper, ed., *Pleasure, Preference and Value*, Cambridge University Press, Cambridge, 1983, pp. 1–16.

Mackie, J. L., *Ethics: Inventing the Difference between Right and Wrong*, Penguin, Harmondsworth, 1977

Malebranche, N., *The Search after Truth*, tr. T. M. Lennon & P. J. Olscamp, Ohio State University, Columbus, 1980

Mayr, E., 'The probability of extraterrestrial intelligent life', E. Regis, ed., *Extraterrestrials: science and alien intelligence*, Cambridge University Press, Cambridge, 1985, pp. 23–30

Miles, Leland, *John Colet and the Platonic Tradition*, Allen & Unwin, London, 1961

Miller, B., *From Existence to God*, Routledge, London, 1992

Miskotte, K. H., *When the Gods are Silent*, tr. J. W. Doberstein, Collins, London, 1967

Moltmann, J., *God in Creation*, tr. M. Kohl, SCM Press, London, 1985

Monod, J., *Chance and Necessity*, tr. A. Wainhouse, Collins, London, 1972

Mothersill, M., *Beauty Restored*, Clarendon Press, Oxford, 1984

Muir, E., *Collected Poems 1921–58*, Faber, London, 1960

Murdoch, I., *The Sovereignty of Good*, Cambridge University Press, Cambridge, 1967

Murdoch, I., *Acastos*, Penguin, Harmondsworth, 1987

Murdoch, I., *Metaphysics as a Guide to Morals*, Penguin, Harmondsworth, 1993 (first published 1992)

Naipaul, V. S., *Among the Believers*, Andre Deutsch, London, 1981

Nozick, R., *Philosophical Explanations*, Clarendon Press, Oxford, 1981

Orwell, G., *Nineteen Eighty-Four*, Penguin, Harmondsworth, 1954 (first published 1949)

Paturi, F. R., *Nature the Mother of Invention*, tr. M. Clarke, Penguin, Harmondsworth, 1978 (first published 1976)

Pearsall Smith, L., *All Trivia*, Constable, London, 1933

Perry, T. D., *Moral Reasoning and Truth*, Clarendon Press, London, 1976

Philo of Alexandria, *Collected Works*, tr. F. H. Colson, G. H. Whitaker *et al.*, Heinemann Loeb Classical Library, London, 1929–62

Pigden, C. R., 'Geach on Good', *Philosophical Quarterly* 40.1990, pp. 129–54.

Plotinus, *Enneads*, tr. S. Mackenna, Faber, London, 1956

Plotinus, *Enneads*, tr. A. H. Armstrong, Heinemann Loeb Classical Library, London, 1966–88

Prior, A., 'Identifiable Individuals', *Review of Metaphysics* 13.1960, pp. 684–6 (reprinted in his *Papers on Time and Tense*, Clarendon Press, Oxford, 1968, pp. 59–77)

Raine, K., *The Inner Journey of the Poet*, Allen & Unwin, London, 1982
Ramsey, F. P., *Foundations of Mathematics*, Kegan Paul, London, 1931
Rist, J. M., *Plotinus: the Road to Reality*, Cambridge University Press, Cambridge, 1967
Ritchie, D. G., *Darwinism and Politics*, Swan Sonnescheen & Co., London 1891 (2nd edn)
Robinson, H. M., *Matter and Sense*, Cambridge University Press, Cambridge, 1982
Rollin, B. *The Unheeded Cry*, Oxford University Press, New York, 1989
Rorty, R. M., *Philosophy and the Mirror of Nature*, Blackwell, Oxford, 1980
Rorty, R. M., *Consequences of Pragmatism*, University of Minnesota Press, Minneapolis, 1982
Ross, G. M., 'Angels', *Philosophy* 60.1985, pp. 495–511

Sextus Empiricus, *Works*, tr. R. G. Bury, Heinemann Loeb Classical Library, London, 1933
Shestov, L., *Potestas Clavium*, tr. B. Martin, Ohio University Press, Athens, Ohio, 1968 (1st edn 1923)
Sircello, G., *A New Theory of Beauty*, Princeton University Press, Princeton & London, 1975
Spencer, H., *The Data of Ethics*, Williams & Norgate, London, 1907
Spinoza, B., *The Ethics and Selected Letters*, tr. S. Shirley, ed. S. Feldman, Hackett, Indianapolis, 1982
Stevens, P. S., *Patterns in Nature*, Penguin, Harmondsworth, 1976
Stout, J., *Ethics since Babel*, James Clarke & Co., Cambridge, 1990

Taylor, C., *Sources of the Self*, Cambridge University Press, Cambridge, 1989
Thucydides, *The History of the Peloponnesian War*, tr. R. W. Livingstone, Oxford University Press, London, 1943

Valentine, C. W., *The Experimental Psychology of Beauty*, Methuen, London, 1962
Vico, G., *On the Ancient Wisdom*, tr. L. H. Palmer, Cornell University Press, Ithaca & London, 1988
Von Uexkuell, J., *Theoretical Biology*, tr. D. L. Mackinnon, Kegan Paul, London, 1926

Walicki, A., *Philosophy and Romantic Nationalism*, Clarendon Press, Oxford, 1982

Ward, M., *Gilbert Keith Chesterton*, Sheed & Ward, London, 1944

Wiley, B., *The Seventeenth-Century Background*, Chatto & Windus, London, 1934

Wittgenstein, L. von, *Notebooks (1914–16)*, Blackwell, Oxford, 1961

Yeats, W. B., *Collected Poems*, Macmillan, London, 1950

NOTES

1 Religious Observances and Theories

1 Amongst other noted modern atheists, Dawkins (1986) and Atkins (1981) are both zealots for their faith, and as inclined as any early Church Father to excoriate anyone who disagrees with them.

2 That is, those who think that 'being true' is only 'being what we say', and 'knowledge' is only approved utterance.

3 Muir 1960, p. 207.

4 Kenny 1979, p. 129.

5 A. H. Clough 'There is no God': Gardner 1972, pp. 684f.

6 *Udana* 8.3: Goddard 1970, p. 32.

7 Aphrodite, as the Greeks knew very well, could evoke courage, awe and tenderness – but also savage cruelty, prurient curiosity and treason. She is not God.

8 Chesterton 1933, p. 128.

9 Herbert 'The Elixir': 1961, p. 175.

10 Berkeley, *Alciphron* (1732) (Euphranor speaks): *Works* vol. 3, p. 297.

11 Berkeley, *Alciphron* (Euphranor speaks): *Works* vol. 3, p. 298. The term 'minute philosopher' is taken by Berkeley's Euphanor, from Seneca, to mean 'the sort of sect which diminish all the most valuable things, the thoughts, views, and hopes of men' (*Alciphron*: *Works* vol. 3, p. 46).

12 Berkeley, *Sermon on the Mission of Christ* (1714): *Works* vol. 7, p. 48.

13 Berkeley, *Sermon on Religious Zeal* (1709–12): *Works* vol. 7, p. 16.

14 Berkeley, *Anniversary S.P.G. Sermon* (1732): *Works* vol. 7, p. 116.

15 Berkeley, *Sermon on Immortality* (1708): *Works* vol. 7, p. 12.

16 Berkeley, *Anniversary S.P.G. Sermon*: *Works* vol. 7, pp. 127f.

17 'The believer may expect a happyness large as our desires, & those desires not stinted to ye few objects we at present receive from some dull inlets of perception, but proportionately to wt our faculties shall be wn God has given the finishing touches to our natures & made us fit inhabitants for heaven' (Berkeley, *Sermon on Immortality*: *Works* vol. 7, p. 12).

18 Apuleius *Metamorphoses* 11.5: Apuleius 1975.

19 Blake *Descriptive Catalogue* no. 3: Blake 1966, p. 567.

20 Blake *Descriptive Catalogue* no. 3: Blake 1966, p. 571.

21 Chiefly, the four noble truths: all is *dukkha*; desire is the root cause of *dukkha*; the ending of desire ends *dukkha*; the eightfold path is the way

to end desire. What those truths mean, in practice and in theory, has taken many centuries, and volumes, to explore.

22 John of Damascus, cited by Lossky 1957, p. 36.
23 Murdoch 1993, p. 508.
24 I have explored the environmental implications of the Sabbath in Clark 1993a.
25 Clark 1989a, p. 150.
26 These aren't identical: neither empiricism in general nor scientific discovery in particular supports 'scientific materialism' – but that is another story.

2   Philosophy and the Betrayal of Thought

1 Augustine *De Libero Arbitrio* 2.7: Augustine 1968, p. 114; Plautus *Amphitruo* 441–7 (Sosio speaks): cited by G. Vico 1988, p. 54. Descartes implies, in a letter to Colvius dated 14 November 1640, that he had not known of Augustine's argument till Colvius mentioned it (Descartes 1970, pp. 83f), adding that he made a different use of what 'could have occurred to any writer'. Actually Augustine made just the same use of the argument (to establish that we were essentially thinking things) in *The Trinity* (Augustine 1963, p. 309: Book 10, ch. 10).
2 'Since I cannot consciously deny that I am thinking, I must concede that I exist.'
3 Otherwise known, perhaps, as the doctrine of *anatta*, the claim that all *dharmas* are empty.
4 Lehrer 1970–1; see Clark 1984, pp. 23f.
5 Nozik 1981, pp. 204ff.
6 Sextus Empiricus *Against the Professors* 7.157: Long & Sedley 1987: vol. I, p. 255 (41C).
7 Rorty 1980, p. 10.
8 If I capitalize 'Truth' it is not to beg any question about its nature, but only to distinguish it at a glance from the anti-realists' 'truth' (which is only what we choose to say).
9 Orwell 1954, p. 241.
10 Sextus Empiricus *Outlines of Pyrrhonism* 1.23: 1933, p. 17.
11 Chesterton 1923a, pp. 176f.
12 Chesterton 'The Blue Cross': 1929, p. 27.
13 Chesterton 1932, p. 126.
14 Ward 1944, p. 526.
15 Chesterton 1933, p. 199.
16 Chesterton 1933, p. 216.
17 Chesterton 1933, pp. 106f.
18 Cupitt 1971, p. 43: that Cupitt later changed his mind is unfortunate.

19 Orwell 1954, p. 68. The preceding sentence ('They [the Party intellec-
tuals] were wrong and he was right!') echoes the Chanson de Roland:
'Païens ont tort. Chrétiens ont droit!'.
20 Berkeley, *Philosophical Commentaries* 676: *Works* vol. 1, p. 82.
21 Berkeley, *Alciphron* (Euphanor speaks): *Works* vol. 3, p. 240.
22 See Berkeley, *Alciphron* (Euphranor speaks): *Works* vol. 3, pp. 257f.
23 Berkeley, *Sermon on the Mission of Christ*: *Works* vol. 7, p. 41.
24 Cupitt 1980, p. 12.
25 Stout 1990, p. 257 (my italics).
26 Robinson 1982, p. 82.
27 Cupitt 1990, p. 183. Cupitt's own instincts, no doubt, are thoroughly
humane; his argument is still confused.
28 Satan speaks: J. Milton *Paradise Lost* 1. 250–6.
29 'To know and not to know, to be conscious of complete truthfulness
while telling carefully constructed lies, to hold simultaneously two
opinions which cancelled out...; to use logic against logic, to repudiate
morality while laying claim to it...; to forget whatever was necessary
to forget, then to draw it back into memory again at the moment when
it was needed, and then promptly to forget it again...': Orwell 1954,
pp. 31f; see also p. 171.
30 Orwell 1954, pp. 45f. 'As the Party slogan put it: "Proles and animals
are free."': ibid., p. 61. 'Syme' is the name of the hero of Chesterton's
The Man who was Thursday.
31 Gabriel Gale speaks: Chesterton 1962, pp. 91f. A similar suggestion is
made by Gabriel Syme in *The Man who was Thursday* (Chesterton
1937, p. 185).
32 Yeats 1950, p. 37.
33 Buchan 'Stocks and Stones': 1923, p. 162.
34 Naipaul 1981, p. 354.
35 Goldstein's *Book*: Orwell 1954, p. 167. Big Brother's face, by the way,
is 'black-haired, black-moustachio'd, full of power and mysterious
calm, and so vast that it almost filled up the screen': Orwell 1954, p. 16.

3 Truth Transcending Thought

1 Plato *Gorgias* 484 c 5ff.
2 I owe this and other references to Ross 1985.
3 Thomas Aquinas, *Summa theologiae* I, q. 52, art. 3.
4 Cited by Wiley 1934, p. 181.
5 See Pearsall Smith 1933, p. 47. See also Ritchie 1891, p. 22: 'the ideas
which rise in the minds of men with the same tendency to variation that

we find throughout nature, compete with one another for sustenance and strength'.

6 Descartes 1931: I, 86.
7 Chesterton 1947, p. 183.
8 Philo *Legum Allegoriae* 2.56.
9 R. Descartes *Dedication to the Meditations*: 1931: I, 133.
10 Epictetus 1926: *Discourses* 3.21.18.
11 Epictetus 1926: *Discourses* 3.21.17.
12 Epictetus 1926: *Discourses* 1.1.25.
13 Boethius 1973: *Discourses* 3.9.8.
14 Epictetus 1926: *Discourses* 4.1.173.
15 Epictetus 1926: *Discourses* 2.9.21.
16 Epictetus 1926: *Encheiridion* 51.3.
17 Cupitt 1980, p. 92.
18 Maximus 11.10b: cited by Dodds 1965, pp. 92f; see also Plotinus *Enneads* V.1.
19 Augustine *The Trinity* 10.8, 11: 1963; see Holscher 1986, p. 129.
20 Berkeley *Philosophical Commentaries* (1707–8) 429: *Works*, vol. 1, p. 53.
21 Augustine *Confessions* 4.7: Holscher 1986, p. 132. Aristotle's notion of an intellect that is eternally active (*De Anima* 3.430) may possibly mean much the same.
22 Augustine *De Libero Arbitrio* 1.24: 1968, p. 95.
23 Plato *Meno* 80e ff.
24 Augustine *Confessions* 10.18: 1961, p. 224.
25 Herbert 1937, pp. 83ff.
26 See Holbrook 1973, pp. 102f.
27 G. M. Hopkins 'Parmenides' (1868): Hopkins 1959, p. 127; for some discussion of Hopkins' terminology see Cotter 1972, and Clark 1990, pp. 108ff.
28 Augustine *De Libero Arbitrio* 2.13.35: 1968, p. 144.
29 Malebranche 1980, p. 234 (3.2.6).
30 Plotinus *Enneads* VI.9.5, 39ff.
31 These alternative descriptions are offered, by Spinoza, as distinct attributes of the one Truth: this is not quite to say that God (that is, the Truth) is simultaneously Matter and Mind, though we must agree at once that whatever Matter and Mind may be must be contained in Truth.
32 Democritos: Kirk, Raven & Schofield 1983, pp. 410ff.
33 Gregory of Nyssa, PG 44: cited by Dodds 1965, p. 11.
34 Heracleitos: Diels & Krantz 1952, 22 B 89.
35 Stobaeus 2.68, 18: Long & Sedley 1987: 1, 256 (41I).
36 Marcus Aurelius *Meditations* 2.17.1.

37 Augustine *De Libero Arbitrio* 2.43: 1968, p. 153.
38 Chesterton 1932, p. 36.
39 Chesterton 1917, p. 59: Heidegger makes a similar connection between thinking and thanking (Heidegger 1968, pp. 138ff).
40 Chesterton 'Ecclesiastes': 1950, p. 326.
41 Buchan 'Stocks and Stones': 1923, p. 161.
42 Pearsall Smith 1933, p. 48.
43 Keats 'Lamia': 1970, p. 176.
44 Keats 'Lamia' (Apollonius speaks): 1970, p. 178.
45 Monod 1972, p. 163.
46 Lewis 1945, p. 411.
47 Orwell 1954, p. 159.
48 Murdoch 1987, p. 101.
49 Descartes 1931: I, xvi. Elizabeth (1618–80) ended as abbess of a Lutheran abbey at Hervorden in Westphalia (see Haldane 1905, p. 267).
50 Descartes 1970, p. 137.
51 Hopkins 1981, p. 20, after Nicholas of Cusa.
52 Orwell 1954, p. 51.
53 Orwell 1954, p. 216.
54 ' "Always there will be the intoxication of power, constantly increasing and constantly growing subtler. Always at every moment, there will be the thrill of victory, the sensation of trampling on an enemy who is helpless" ': O'Brien speaks, Orwell 1954, p. 215.
55 Orwell 1954, p. 233.
56 Orwell 1954, p. 102.
57 Orwell 1954, p. 176.
58 Orwell 1954, p. 215. The same prophecy was made by Wickson in Jack London's *The Iron Heel* (1934), pp. 94f. London's future history is very like Orwell's: what Orwell realized was that the organization of Revolutionary Fighting Groups (ibid., pp. 220ff) that permeates the organization of the Iron Heel would actually serve the Heel's purposes, and that Socialism itself would serve as the overt ideology of the oppressors (as the Foreign Workers Press so lamentably failed to see). P. Vaillant-Couturier's complacent praise, in the introduction to the Foreign Worker's edition, of the USSR as 'a revolutionary people that nothing can vanquish because it is armed with a correct doctrine, applied in a consistent manner by a disciplined Party, with the enlightened and enthusiastic support of the masses' is a reminder that Orwell did not have to invent Ingsoc.
59 Orwell 1954, p. 176.
60 Orwell, ibid.
61 Orwell 1954, p. 86.

62 Raine 1982, p. 57.
63 Murdoch 1967, p. 85.
64 The crass literal-mindedness of those who calculate how large a breastbone a winged humanoid would need is a particularly extreme example of the failure of the philosophical imagination in this century.
65 Chesterton 1961, p. 20.

4   Necessity and Unity

1 The point is made at greater length by Miller 1992, pp. 79ff.
2 The claim is argued by Jonathan Edwards, and picked up by Prior 1960.
3 Terry Pratchett is a deservedly popular comic writer, specializing in parodies of more serious-minded fantasy and science fiction: Discworld is a flat, inhabited disc resting on four elephants upon the back of a gigantic turtle!
4 So realizing, in reverse, one of Zeno's paradoxes: to achieve the target an arrow must pass successively through half, a quarter, an eighth, a sixteenth (and so forever) of the remaining distance. How then, he asked, could the arrow reach the target? One plausible answer is that the arrow can pass through those infinitely many distances because it has, on the same terms, infinitely many moments to accomplish it. The cosmos may have begun a finite time ago (in years accomplished) and still have experienced infinitely many discriminable moments since 'the start'.
5 See Craig 1979, and Craig & Smith 1993 for further analysis of the difficulties with temporal beginnings, and their absence.
6 See, for example, Atkins 1981.
7 Edwards 1966, pp. 45f.
8 Edwards 1966, p. 51.
9 The suggestion is that twinned particles, created in an instant, will continue to mirror each other's changes however far they travel. By engineering a change in one, we guarantee a matching change elsewhere – except, of course, that no one could read that change.
10 Muir 1960, p. 207.
11 Malebranche 1980, p. 251 (3.2.9).

5   Having the Mind of God

1 Augustine *The Trinity* 4.1: 1963, p. 130.
2 Edwards 1966, p. 48: as Parmenides also said (Kirk, Raven & Schofield 1983, p. 246: Fr.28 B 3DK, after Plotinus, *Enneads* V.1.8).
3 Malebranche 1980, p. 251 (3.2.9).

4 Augustine *On Christian Doctrine* 1.7f: 1958, p. 12.
5 Aristotle *Nicomachean Ethics* 10.1177a12ff; *Metaphysics* 12.1072b13f.
6 Cleanthes speaks: Hume, 'Dialogues': 1963, p. 133.
7 Augustine *The Trinity* 1.1: 1963, p. 4. Descartes 1983, p. 23 (Part 1.51): 'the term "substance" does not apply to God and to those other things "univocally".'
8 Strictly, Plotinus distinguishes (*Enneads* V.5.12, 9ff) the good (*agathon*) and the beautiful (*kalon*), but Armstrong's equation is allowable.
9 Plotinus *Enneads* V.1.11.
10 Plotinus *Enneads* V.9.5.
11 Plotinus *Enneads* V.3.5, 23-4.
12 Plotinus *Enneads* IV.4.12.
13 Plotinus *Enneads* V.9.5.31f, after Aristotle *De Anima* 3.430a3ff.
14 Plotinus *Enneads* V.9.13, 9f.
15 Plotinus *Enneads* V.9.8, 4f.
16 Plotinus *Enneads* V.8.4.
17 Plotinus *Enneads* V.5.1, 54ff.
18 Plotinus *Enneads* V.3.5, 23ff.
19 Plotinus *Enneads* V.5.2, 18–20.
20 Plotinus *Enneads* V.3.3, 46ff.
21 Plotinus *Enneads* VI.7.13, 28f.
22 Augustine *Confessions* 13.25: 1961, p. 337.
23 Augustine *De Libero Arbitrio* 3.13: 1968, p. 177.
24 Chesterton 1925, pp. 293f.
25 Chesterton 1923b, p. 95.
26 Hopkins 1967, p. 90.
27 Geach 1968, p. 15.
28 Which is why the merely Platonic answer to the earlier puzzle about coming-to-be amounts to the same thing as theism: 'independent natures' exist as the thoughts of God.
29 On which see Clark 1996a.
30 Haldane 1934, p. 64.
31 And see Augustine *Confessions* 13.38: 1961, p. 346: 'We see the things which you [God] have made, because they exist. But they only exist because you see them.'
32 Plotinus *Enneads* V.1.2, 10–27.
33 Plato *Phaedrus* 245c9; Plotinus *Enneads* V.1.2, 9.
34 Berkeley, *Philosophical Commentaries* 392: *Works* vol. 1, p. 47.
35 Malebranche 1980 (1.14.1), p. 67; see also p. 217.
36 Herbert 1937, p. 329.

6   The Beautiful and True

1 Paturi 1978, p. 67.
2 Paturi 1978, p. 52.
3 Paturi 1978, p. 53.
4 Valentine 1962, pp. 93f.
5 Chandrasekhar 1987, p. 52, quoting Freeman Dyson's quotation of Weyl. Compare Dostoyevsky's preference for Christ over the true, or the provably true, in Dostoyevsky 1962, p. 71.
6 Cited by Gleick 1987, p. 117.
7 Aristotle *Poetics* 1450b7f *et al.*
8 Chesterton 1961, p. 64.
9 Plotinus *Enneads* VI.7.22, 24–31.
10 See Sircello 1975, pp. 81ff; also Clark 1993c.
11 Plotinus *Enneads* I.6.4: 1956, p. 59 (as a general rule, Armstrong's translation of Plotinus has to be preferred, but there is a particular charm in McKenna's, on occasion).
12 Eco 1986, p. 22: strictly, Plotinus distinguishes Beauty (which is equivalent to Being) and the Good (which is to say, the One) - but that is a distinction which need not concern us here.
13 Bernard *Sermones in Cantica* 25, 6: cited by Eco 1986, p. 9.
14 Blake 1966, p. 447.
15 Darwin 1981, vol. 1, pp. 71f.
16 Darwin 1981, p. 97.
17 Thucydides 1943, p. 190: 3.82.
18 Spencer 1907, p. 114: see Darwin 1981, p. 101, referring to 'our great philosopher'.
19 See Aristotle *Eudemian Ethics* 8.1248b25f.
20 As I pointed out, *contra* Midgley, in Clark 1980.
21 Darwin 1981, p. 73. See F. Herbert, *Hellstrom's Hive* (Nelson Double-day Inc: New York, 1973) for a fictional attempt to depict such a society.
22 Those who attempt the task often seem not to understand what it is that they have lost: see Clark 1989b.
23 Darwin 1981, p. 70: 'conscience ... [is] the most noble of the attributes of man'.
24 Darwin 1981, pp. 94, 101.
25 Aristotle *Politics* 7.1332a20f.
26 Aristotle *Eudemian Ethics* 8.1249b20.
27 Stevens 1976, p. 166. Mothersill 1984, pp. 125ff discusses Fibonacci and the Golden Section, unsympathetically.
28 Ramsey 1931, p. 291. Von Uexkuell 1926, pp. 35ff says the same.
29 McDowell 1983.

30 Chandrasekhar 1987, p. 66.
31 A point I argued in an early paper, Clark 1977.
32 Anscombe 1981, pp. ixf.
33 Anscombe, *Socratic Digest* 1947: Anscombe 1981, pp. 224–32.
34 'Priests have always used their power to evade the moral obligations of the ordinary man' (Haldane 1930, p. 247). Oddly, Haldane himself also insists that 'the average man ... must learn that the highest of his duties is to assist those who are creating, and the worst of his sins is to hinder them' (ibid., p. 311): that is to say, the clerks of Haldane's own religion are to evade the obligations of the ordinary man.
35 Haldane 1934, p. 51.
36 Chesterton 1961, p. 33.
37 Haldane 1930, p. 235.
38 Mayr 1985, p. 28.
39 Monod 1972, p. 160.

7 Decency and Moral Truth

1 Unless our own 'best image' is so far corrupt as to require mending: maybe in unfallen creatures that best image is identical with what the creature is itself, in God; in fallen creatures like ourselves, we may be disconnected even from our selves.
2 Plutarch *On common conceptions* 1076a: Long & Sedley 1987, vol. 1, p. 380: 61J: Dion is Everyman – but the name is cognate with the root of 'Zeus'.
3 This is to take the view that individual scientists (and scholars and philosophers) should seek to practice what they preach, as individuals: it is only fair to add that, people being what they are, there may be reason instead to prefer an institutional response. Instead of relying on individual virtue, we may hope that individual vices (of envy, malice and ambition) can be harnessed to the service of civil peace and intellectual progress. Churches don't necessarily require saints: they may even rather dislike them.
4 Aristotle *Nicomachean Ethics* 10.1177b19ff; *Metaphysics* 12.1072b26ff.
5 Aristotle *Nicomachean Ethics* 10.1178b8ff; Plotinus *Enneads* VI.8.5.
6 Hooykaas, after Cotes' preface to the second edition of Newton's *Principia* (Hooykaas 1972, p. 49). Hooykaas continues, unjustly, 'the first thrust is levelled at the Greeks, the second at Descartes'. Unjustly, because 'the Greeks' were not uniformly sceptical, and Descartes expressly disavowed the possibility of second-guessing God: 'seeing that [the parts into which matter is divided] could have been regulated

by God in an infinity of diverse ways, experience alone should teach us which of all these ways He chose' (Descartes 1983, p. 106 (Part 3.46)).

7   There could be an infinite array even though most possible worlds did not exist at all: maybe only one in a googol (10^{100}) worlds exists – and why should any of them be life-bearing ones?

8   Which I have discussed at greater length in Clark 1998.

9   Lucretius *On the Nature of Things* 4.830ff: Long & Sedley 13E: vol. 1, p. 58.

10 Plutarch *On Stoic Self-contradictions* 1044d: Long & Sedley 54O, vol. 1, p. 328.

11 'Superior civilizations' have 'an historic right' to tear 'the splendid land of California from the lazy Mexicans': cited by Walicki 1982, p. 376.

12 Spinoza *Ethics*, Part I, Appendix, p. 58.

13 Descartes 1983, p. 14; cf. 'We cannot know God's purposes unless God reveals them' (Descartes 1970, p. 117).

14 As Perry 1976 shows.

15 Taylor 1989, p. 160; see pp. 186f.

16 Lewis 1946, p. 49.

17 Aristotle *De Partibus Animalium* 1.645b17.

18 Spinoza 3p7: p. 109.

19 Spinoza himself fell back, like the Stoics, into the anthropocentric error of supposing that the good of other, non-human creatures might justly be neglected (Spinoza 4p37: p. 175; 4p68s: p. 193) because *their* goods are of less importance, to us, than ours.

20 Wittgenstein 1961: 2 September 1916.

21 Chesterton 1961, p. 21.

22 Wittgenstein 1961: 26 October 1916.

23 Chesterton 1923b, pp. 29ff.

24 Chesterton 1923b, p. 39.

25 The distinction between the One and Intellect is real: Intellect (or Being or Beauty) itself 'looks back' to what we call the One. Conversely, the manifold-in-unity which is that Intellect is an expression of that One which transcends even Intellect. Plotinus is our best guide to the philosophical arguments for the position.

26 See Clark 1991, pp. 79ff. The point may be the one that Mersenne suggested to Descartes: see Descartes 1970, p. 14.

27 Evans-Pritchard 1956, pp. 124ff; Heinrich Heine had made the same distinction (though with what seems, superficially, the opposite implication): 'everything is not God; God is everything' (1835), cited by Moltmann 1985, p. 103.

28 Berkeley, *Alciphron* (Crito speaks): *Works* vol. 3, pp. 251f.

29 Berkeley, *Alciphron* (Euphranor speaks): *Works* vol. 3, p. 128.

30 Descartes 1983, p. 36 (Part I.76).

31 Augustine *On Christian Doctrine* (prologue 4) 1958, p. 4.
32 Descartes 1983, p. 36 (Part 1.76).
33 Descartes 1970, p. 11 (to Mersenne, 15 April 1630).
34 Shestov 1968, p. 341.
35 See Clark 1982; 1987.

8 Communities of Faith

1 Berkeley, *Sermon on Immortality*: *Works* vol. 7, p. 14.
2 Berkeley, *Sermon on Immortality*: *Works* vol. 7, p. 14; see also vol. 3, p. 143.
3 Augustine *De Libero Arbitrio* 3.59: 1968, p. 219. See also Descartes 1983, p. 85 (Part 3.3) on the benefits – and perils – of believing that the world was made 'for us'.
4 Descartes 1983, p. 106 (Part 3.46): 'seeing that [the parts into which matter is divided] could have been regulated by God in an infinity of diverse ways, experience alone should teach us which of all these ways He chose'.
5 On the one hand nothing really matters; on the other, anyone who thinks that we don't matter more than anything else is mad.
6 Berkeley, *Letter to Sir John James* (1741): *Works* vol. 7, p. 147.
7 Berkeley, *Sermon on Religious Zeal*: *Works*, vol. 7, p. 20.
8 Herbert 1937, p. 72.
9 Miles 1961, pp. 128, 141.
10 Philo *Legum Allegoriae* 2.56 vol. 2, p. 259. See also Plotinus *Enneads* 1.6.7, 5–7, and Rist 1967, pp. 188–98.
11 Berkeley, *Siris* (1744) 313f: *Works* vol. 5, p. 145, citing Proclus' Commentary on Alcibiades I, after Plato's *Republic* 10.611cff; see also Plotinus *Enneads* 1.1.12.
12 Berkeley, *Siris* 296: *Works* vol. 5, p. 137.
13 Berkeley, *Guardian Essay on the Pineal Gland* (1713): *Works* vol. 7, p. 191: compare Cupitt's claim that anyone who accepts the God of objective metaphysical theism is 'anti-intellectual, arrogant, bigoted, self-deceived and self-regarding' (Cupitt 1980, p. 83), and 'belongs with the more backward countries of the Third World and the socialistic block' (Cupitt 1980, p. 17). Cupitt was apparently writing with no ironical intention.
14 Berkeley, *Alciphron* (Alciphron speaks): *Works* vol. 3, p. 39; see pp. 34f.
15 Berkeley, *Discourse to Magistrates* (1738): *Works* vol. 6, pp. 203f.
16 Boswell 1953, p. 361 (Spring 1766): Johnson replied, 'Why, yes, Sir; and what then? This now is such stuff as I used to talk to my mother,

when I first began to think myself a clever fellow; and she ought to have whipt me for it.'

17 Berkeley, *Siris* 232f: *Works* vol. 5, p. 111.
18 Berkeley, *Alciphron* (Euphranor speaks): *Works* vol. 3, p. 59; cf. *Alciphron* (Alciphron speaks): *Works*, vol. 3, p. 221.
19 Berkeley, *Letter to Sir John James*: *Works* vol. 7, p. 148.
20 Berkeley, *Letter to Sir John James*: *Works* vol. 7, p. 146. Further pejorative remarks on popery occur in *Alciphron* (*Works* vol. 3, pp. 78f, 109f, 195, 209), and in his letters to the Roman clergy of Ireland (*Works* vol. 6, pp. 229-49).
21 Chesterton 1961, p. 32.
22 Berkeley, *Primary Visitation Charge* (1734–7): *Works* vol. 7, p. 163.
23 Berkeley, *Letter to Sir John James*: *Works* vol. 7, p. 145; see *Alciphron* (Euphranor speaks): *Works* vol. 3, p. 226.
24 Berkeley, *Siris* 264: *Works* vol. 5, p. 124.
25 Berkeley, *Guardian Essay on Pleasures*: *Works* vol. 7, pp. 194f.
26 Augustine *De Libero Arbitrio* 2.41: 1968, p. 151.
27 Berkeley, *Discourse to Magistrates*: *Works* vol. 7, p. 217 (my italics).
28 Berkeley, *Sermon on the Mystery of Godliness* (1731): *Works* vol. 7, p. 91.
29 Herbert 1937, p. 120.
30 Herbert 1937, p. 131.
31 Berkeley, *Alciphron* (Euphranor speaks): *Works* vol. 3, p. 143.
32 Berkeley, *Siris* 339: *Works* vol. 5, p. 154.
33 Berkeley, *Alciphron* (Euphranor speaks): *Works* vol. 3, p. 255.
34 Berkeley, *Discourse to Magistrates*: *Works* vol. 6, p. 217.
35 Berkeley, *Letter to Samuel Johnson* (1729): *Works* vol. 2, p. 282.
36 Especially if no free-thinker will accept an axiom from which God's existence follows.
37 Berkeley, *Alciphron* (Euphranor speaks): *Works* vol. 3, p. 296.
38 Berkeley, *The Analyst* (1734): *Works* vol. 4, p. 69.
39 Berkeley, *Alciphron* (Euphranor speaks): *Works* vol. 3, p. 298.
40 Berkeley, *Alciphron* (Euphranor speaks): *Works* vol. 3, p. 229.
41 Berkeley, *Alciphron* (Crito speaks): *Works* vol. 3, p. 241: 'By common sense ... should be meant, either the general sense of mankind, or the improved reason of thinking men.'
42 Berkeley, *Alciphron* (Euphranor speaks): *Works* vol. 3, p. 314: 'walking before them was thought the proper way to confute those ingenious men [who undertook to prove that motion was impossible].'
43 Berkeley, *Alciphron* (Euphranor speaks): *Works* vol. 3, p. 299.
44 Berkeley, *Works* vol. 3, p. 297.
45 Berkeley, *Alciphron*: *Works*, vol. 3, p. 46, after Cicero *De Senectute* 86.

46 Berkeley, *Alciphron* (Crito speaks): *Works*, vol. 3, p. 322: Crito's argument is to a slightly different point.
47 O'Brien speaks: Orwell 1954, p. 214.
48 O'Brien speaks: Orwell 1954, p. 197: see also, after Winston's psychological destruction, p. 238.
49 Orwell 1954, p. 68.
50 Orwell 1954, p. 52.
51 Orwell 1954, p. 184.
52 See Orwell 1954, pp. 28, 102.
53 O'Brien speaks, in the Ministry of Love: Orwell 1954, p. 204.
54 Orwell 1954, p. 208.

9 The Last Things

1 Lovejoy 1930, p. 14.
2 See Clark 1993c and my 'How and Why to be Virtuous': *The Personalist Review*, forthcoming.
3 Berkeley, *Discourse to Magistrates*: *Works* vol. 6, p. 206; see my essay on 'Berkeley's Philosophy of Religion' in K. Winkler, ed., *Companion to Berkeley* (Cambridge: Cambridge University Press), forthcoming.
4 Chesterton 1946, p. 64.
5 Chesterton 1950, p. 268. Orwell identifies (Orwell 1954, p. 5) the poem that 'the poet Ampleforth' cannot correct for the Ministry of Truth (involving a rhyme of 'rod' and 'God') with one of Kipling's: I suspect he misremembered –

For riseth up against realm and rod,
A thing forgotten, a thing downtrod,
The last, lost giant, even God,
Is risen against the world.

6 Orwell 1954, p. 23.
7 Rorty 1982, p. xlii. See Stout 1990, p. 257. Stout goes on to say, contra Rorty, that *he* and 'the example of every remaining virtuous person, as well as whatever exemplary lives we can keep alive in memory' can still condemn the torturer (ibid., p. 259). But that is to miss Orwell's point.
8 Augustine 1963, p. 9.
9 Aristotle *Nicomachean Ethics* 6.1144a34f: the more usual, and perhaps more accurate, translation is 'wickedness makes us make mistakes about the principles of action'.
10 Konyndyk 1995, p. 19.
11 See Aristotle *Rhetoric* 3.1411b12.
12 Cicero *On Divination* 1.82f, 117f: Long & Sedley 1987, 42Dff. The

argument is offered in defence of divination: it is a better defence of scientific inference than is now common.

13 There is one further twist, to adopt an openly polytheistic metaphysics, in which opposing values all make their demands, and take their cut. Such polytheism is what the poet Yeats expected, and too many moderns have delivered: see Clark 1989a, pp. 29ff.

14 Moses, in the Yiddish joke, on the return down Sinai: 'First the good news: I got Him down to ten. Now the bad: adultery is still in.'

15 Dale 1982, p. 107.

16 Chesterton 1929, pp. 104ff.

17 Auden 1966, p. 84.

18 Chesterton 1929, p. 124.

19 Chesterton 1927, p. 18.

20 I have examined various recipes for immortality in Clark 1995a.

21 Keats, 'Ode to a Grecian Urn': 1956, p. 210.

22 Haldane 1934, p. 58.

23 Cardenal 1974, p. 40.

24 Julian (chapter 5) 1966, p. 68; see Murdoch 1993, pp. 485f.

25 See Leslie 1996.

26 Even the notion that there *are* such creatures depends upon the belief that our human intellects are especially appropriate forms of life: if theism were false, this would be astonishingly unlikely – a point I have argued in Clark 1994.

27 Kallen 1969, pp. 17ff.

28 See Miskotte 1967, pp. 155f.

29 Augustine *De Libero Arbitrio* 2.13.35: 1968, p. 4.

30 Berry 1991, p. 139.

Index

The Society for Promoting Christian Knowledge (SPCK) has as its purpose three main tasks:

- **Communicating the Christian faith in its rich diversity**
- **Helping people to understand the Christian faith and to develop their personal faith**
- **Equipping Christians for mission and ministry**

SPCK Worldwide serves the Church through Christian literature and communication projects in over 100 countries. Special schemes also provide books for those training for ministry in many parts of the developing world. SPCK Worldwide's ministry involves Churches of many traditions. This worldwide service depends upon the generosity of others and all gifts are spent wholly on ministry programmes, without deductions.

SPCK Bookshops support the life of the Christian community by making available a full range of Christian literature and other resources, and by providing support to bookstalls and book agents throughout the UK. SPCK Bookshops' mail order department meets the needs of overseas customers and those unable to have access to local bookshops.

SPCK Publishing produces Christian books and resources, covering a wide range of inspirational, pastoral, practical and academic subjects. Authors are drawn from many different Christian traditions, and publications aim to meet the needs of a wide variety of readers in the UK and throughout the world.

The Society does not necessarily endorse the individual views contained in its publications, but hopes they stimulate readers to think about and further develop their Christian faith.

For further information about the Society, please write to:

SPCK, Holy Trinity Church, Marylebone Road,
London NW1 4DU, United Kingdom.
Telephone: 0171 387 5282